The Welfare State and Equality

The Welfare State and Equality

STRUCTURAL AND IDEOLOGICAL ROOTS
OF PUBLIC EXPENDITURES

by

Harold L. Wilensky

UNIVERSITY OF CALIFORNIA PRESS

BERKELEY   •   LOS ANGELES   •   LONDON

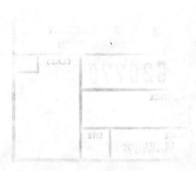

University of California Press
Berkeley and Los Angeles, California
University of California Press, Ltd.
London, England
Copyright © 1975, by
Harold L. Wilensky
ISBN 0-520-02908-9
Library of Congress Catalog Card Number: 74-79146
Printed in the United States of America

3 4 5 6 7 8 9 0

*For my mother
and the memory of my father*

Contents

Tables

Figures

Preface

  This book explores two basic problems in the study of rich (or "post-industrial") societies: first, the interplay of affluence, economic system, political system, and ideology; second, the effect of social organization on the behavior of political elites. The behavior at issue is the allocation of scarce resources to government programs of health, education, welfare, and housing. My main aim is to discover the structural and cultural determinants of the welfare state and to explain why rich countries, having adopted similar health and welfare programs, diverge so sharply in their levels of spending, organization and administration of services and benefits, and styles of administration. I hope also to show how sociologists, as they pursue their central subject, social structure and change, can descend from ponderous abstractions and produce more modest, more concrete propositions about the effect of social organization on behavior.

  For some years I have been trying to understand the reluctance of the United States to join such affluent countries as Sweden, the Netherlands, West Germany, France, and Belgium in the provision of health and welfare benefits and services as a matter of social right. I summarized my views of American "exceptionalism" in an essay, "The Problems and Prospects of the Welfare State" (1965). Aware, however, that the public welfare effort of such affluent countries as Switzerland, Australia, Canada, and Japan was not very different from that of the United States—and eager to overcome my American parochialism in sociological analysis—I began in 1970 to plan a comparative study of the welfare state. The study focuses on variations in the types, budgets, and administration of health and welfare programs and the impact of these programs on real welfare. In order to test theories of convergence of urban-industrial societies—the idea that whatever their political economies, whatever their unique cultures and histories, the "affluent" societies become more alike in both social structure and ideology—I concentrate on public expenditures of rich countries. Because so many scholars and politicians concede that the welfare state achieves a measure of psychological and social security, but question whether it results in a measure of equality, I concentrate on those programs that are egalitarian in their effect on income distribution. Because it is commonly assumed that the two biggest packages of public spending—external security, loosely called "defense," and internal security, loosely labeled "social security"—are in competition for public resources, I pay some attention to the effect of military budgets and wars, big and small, on public civilian expenditures.

The present volume presents the ideas that guide this long-range program of research and reports my initial results. My research strategy for both this book and the larger study is to analyze crude cross-sectional data on gross categories of welfare and military spending for sixty-four countries, to do more detailed time-series analysis of the better data available for the twenty-two richest countries, and then to conduct intensive historical case studies of selected welfare-state leaders, laggards, and middle-rank spenders among the richest countries—to be set in the context of quantitative analysis. Emphasis on the rich countries is not only desirable for testing convergence theory, but necessary because of well-known limitations of data. Rich countries are at once rich in goods and services and rich in data;

statistical records of less affluent countries are, in contrast, quite
weak. Further, even for the rich nations, acceptable data on
trends in social security spending are available for large samples
only from about 1950 to 1966. For the broad sweep of history,
therefore, we must infer the effects of industrialization and
urbanization by comparing rich and poor countries at one
cross-sectional moment, as I do in chapter 2, and by comparing
present and past in selected rich countries.

As a first report, this book examines the welfare state as a
research problem, presents my major research questions and
hypotheses, and outlines problems of method and measurement.
Some preliminary data will guide the discussion; to facilitate the
work of other students, I discuss the uses and limits of these data
in the Appendix.

Here is a preview of the argument. On the basis of a
cross-sectional analysis of sixty-four countries, I conclude that
economic growth and its demographic and bureaucratic outcomes are the root cause of the general emergence of the welfare
state—the establishment of similar programs of social security,
the increasing fraction of GNP devoted to such programs, the
trend toward comprehensive coverage and similar methods of
financing. In any systematic comparison of many countries over
many years, alternative explanations collapse under the weight
of such heavy, brittle categories as "socialist" versus "capitalist"
economies, "collectivistic" versus "individualistic" ideologies, or
even "democratic" versus "totalitarian" political systems. However useful they may be in the understanding of other problems,
these categories are almost useless in explaining the origins and
general development of the welfare state.

At an advanced stage of affluence and in countries matched
for per capita income, however, we find sharp differences in the
organization and level of welfare and in the politics of welfare.
For instance, the student of public spending quickly notes large
differences in the proportion of resources these countries spend
on social security: in 1966, from a range among welfare-state
leaders of about 21 to 16 percent of GNP (Austria to East

Germany); among welfare-state laggards, of 10 to 6 percent (USSR to Japan). Accompanying these differences in welfare effort are momentous differences in administrative organization and style. Even a superficial observer cannot miss the expression in everyday life of divergent national styles. When I was living in Sweden for four months in 1970, I was struck by a debate that surfaced on the front pages of the Stockholm newspapers and on the evening television news. How outrageous it was, said the commentators, that the inclined plane of a certain subway entrance was too steep for the comfort of handicapped Swedes bound to a wheelchair. The situation should be rectified. An American wonders, "Could this become a matter of intensive public controversy in New York City?"

Another minor event symbolized for me these contrasting national styles. In 1972, the government of the Netherlands was experimenting with a new ten-guilder note having three raised Braille dots so that a Dutchman afflicted with blindness would not feel lost in a commercial market. If the idea proved helpful to the blind, it would be adopted nationally for all currency. An American student of welfare might reflect that, although the blind constitute the most appealing and effective lobby of the handicapped in the United States, such a national response is hardly within reach.

In big ways and small, then, the rich countries diverge. I argue in this book that such differences between the welfare-state leaders and laggards can be explained by specific differences in political, social, and economic organization—by the degree of centralization of government, the shape of the stratification order and related mobility rates, the organization of the working class, and the position of the military.

This volume is intended to open the way for more systematic sociological studies of the sources, substance, and effects of the welfare state. On the theoretical side such studies can permit an assessment of a major area of convergence or divergence; on the social problems and public policy side they can illuminate the fate of equality and the impact of military budgets on nonmilitary expenditures. Compared with the topics that preoccupy students of stratification and power structure (occupational mobility, elite recruitment, voter preferences, emerging styles of work and life), or the topics that delight students of social problems (deviance, student rebellion, race relations), the study of pensions and public aid lacks glamour. Yet an analysis of the determinants and effects of such large components of government budgets may be more central to the question of "who gets what, how, and why" than most of the stratification research of recent years.[1]

Some readers may feel that in my sympathy for the underprivileged aged, unemployed, handicapped, and other minorities, I have uncritically embraced all welfare legislation, that I assume "the more the better," that I envision no desirable upper limit to public spending, or that I underestimate the value of private solutions to these public problems.

Although critics of the welfare state are by no means uniform in their ideological stance, we can group most of them, with only a little oversimplification, as "conservative" or "radical." Conservative critics lodge four major complaints. First, if the welfare state does not impoverish the professional and middle classes, it enrages them, turning their support to even more regressive economic policies and more repressive politics. Second, the welfare state rewards the idle and improvident (now including college students), thereby undermining the virtues of thrift, disciplined work, and self-reliance. The old image of "welfare chiselers" driving about in secondhand Cadillacs is still alive. Third, modern welfare systems increase the power of the state. Conservative critics are especially worried by two expressions of statism. Bureaucracies, they say, are arrogant and

---

1. Students of the shape of modern society need a new sociology of knowledge to explain the inverse relation between the political importance of an institutional sphere and the systematic attention sociologists have given to it. The chief candidates for "least studied and most talked about" are the welfare state, the military, the mass media and mass entertainment, and the intellectuals and experts—perhaps the most distinctive marks of modern life.

self-expanding and cannot be reduced when they have outlived their usefulness; the perpetuation of useless, even harmful programs is thus assured. A related pathology of the welfare state is equally dangerous: welfare expenditures undermine both economic freedoms and democratic liberties—the first by "confiscatory taxation," the second by making everyone a dependent client of a bureaucratic state. Finally, the welfare state, conservative critics assert, does not work; it produces neither security nor equality, but merely whets mass appetites that cannot be satisfied.

In recent years, "radical" critics have joined their conservative counterparts with an oddly similar attack. They also denounce statism, but base the charge on a stereotype of the "middle class" bias of the welfare establishment, which they see as an agent of repressive government seeking to transform the poor into pale imitations of bourgeois status-strivers. In their more romantic moods, these radical critics also complain that the welfare state destroys the "subculture of poverty" with its spontaneity, sensuality, informality, and good humor; or, worse, it subverts diverse traditions of ethnic-religious groups, class, or neighborhood. Finally, they write off even participatory programs (such as the U.S. Office of Economic Opportunity's Community Action Program in the 1960s) as "co-optation," the drawing off of protest leadership into futile reform programs that buttress the status quo and divert attention from the necessity of radical change. Like conservatives, they view welfare bureaucrats as policemen—restrictive agents of surveillance and control. Like conservatives, they argue that the welfare state does not work.

I dismiss neither line of criticism as trivial.

Unfortunately, the comparative research that would permit a balanced assessment of these assertions does not exist. And neither conservatives nor radicals have been guided by the data already in hand. With an eye to those data, in my final chapter I shall give my judgment of the critics' arguments. But first we must consider the sources and substance of "the" welfare state and at least glance at the problem of how we might undertake a serious assessment of its effects, short-run and long. For no useful debate about the human value of the welfare state can escape the similarities and differences in national responses to welfare issues. The welfare state comes in assorted forms, variously vulnerable to each line of attack. Perhaps my analysis will bring the critics' target into focus, even if in the end the welfare state in its wondrous diversity proves hard to shoot down.

This book elaborates and tests ideas presented in a plenary session of the 65th Annual Meeting of the American Sociological Association, Washington, D.C., September 1970, and in "The Welfare State, Equality, and War," *Analyse et Prévision*, XV (January 1973), 87–94. It is part of a program of research made possible by the generous support of the National Science Foundation (Grant GS-37084X) and the Institute of International Studies and the Institute of Industrial Relations of the University of California, Berkeley. Where I cite no source the discussion is based on exploratory interviews I conducted in 1970–1972 in ten countries with politicians, welfare administrators, and experts on public spending. I am grateful to Martin A. Trow, Jeffery M. Paige, Eugene A. Hammel, Aaron Wildavsky, Barbara L. Heyns, A. R. Isserlis, and Grant Barnes for critical readings, and to Howard D. White, Paul Lewis, Kathleen Gerson, Peter Enström, Richard M. Coughlin, William P. Carpenter, Robert K. Boggs, and Philip K. Armour for research assistance.

Berkeley, California   HAROLD L. WILENSKY
January 25, 1974

The Welfare State as a
Research Problem

The essence of the welfare state is government-protected minimum standards of income, nutrition, health, housing, and education, assured to every citizen as a political right, not as charity. It is commonly argued that programs to achieve these standards are regressive in their financing and, therefore, have little to do with equality. Evidence suggests, however, that most "social security" programs, although they are typically financed by regressive contributory and tax schemes, produce some income redistribution in their payout, at least in the short run (e.g., national health services, flat-rate pensions, family allowances, public assistance, labor market and manpower programs, rent supplements). Even an earnings-related pension scheme, which preserves among pensioners the income differentials of their working lives, redistributes income from the currently employed to a major group of the poor, the aged. On the whole the welfare state is probably egalitarian in its net effect.

The welfare state is at once one of the great structural uniformities of modern society and, paradoxically, one of its most striking diversities. Scholars impressed by the convergence of urban-industrial societies toward some common "post-industrial" condition can see in every rich country seven or eight

1

health and welfare programs with similar content and expanded
funding—even some convergence in methods of financing and
administration. Students impressed with the vast variety of
"urban-industrial" or "affluent" societies can cite large differences in national effort and organization, in administrative style
and related rhetoric, not to mention apparent contrasts in real
welfare outputs.

To grasp these differences and similarities in national
welfare effort, we must begin with an analysis of "public
consumption expenditures," the concept and accounting con-
vention that comes closest to capturing the idea of the welfare
state. Public consumption expenditures are current expenditures
for goods and services and those transfer payments made by
governments that are financed exclusively through taxation or
public borrowing. The recipients make no direct payment for
what they receive. Excluded are public investment expenditures,
government subsidies, and sales by government agencies to the
population (Pryor, 1968, pp. 26–27). Broader than the transfer
payments usually associated with "welfare" programs, public
consumption expenditures include only two substantial categories that are not clearly devoted to implementing the welfare
state—the military and general administration.

The largest public consumption expenditures are for defense, education, welfare, and health, which together comprise
at least two-thirds of general government expenditures in rich
countries for which we have data.[1] Dominating the "welfare and
health" category are three expensive programs: pensions, death
benefits, disability insurance; sickness and/or maternity benefits
or health insurance or a national health service like Britain's;

1. Based on 1967–1969 average expenditure as a percentage of government
current expenditure for defense, health, and education (excluding welfare) in
eleven of our twenty-two rich countries for which comparable data are available
(OECD, 1972, p. 115, table A6). Since in that table OECD excludes all transfer
payments for welfare, health, and education, this average expenditure—59
percent—is for current goods and services alone. Thus it considerably under-
states public consumption expenditures for defense, health, welfare, education.

and family or child allowances. Also included are the less expensive programs of workmen's compensation or work-injury protection, unemployment compensation, and related labor market policies; "public assistance" or "social assistance" including miscellaneous aid to the handicapped and the poor; and benefits for "war victims." (See the Appendix.) Because research has shown that these health and welfare expenditures form a more or less coherent package and tend to move together, I shall refer to all of them as "welfare programs."

Before tackling the patterns of civilian expenditure labeled "the welfare state" we must set aside education and housing for special consideration—the first for reasons of theory, the second because of severe data limitations. And in a search for the causes of variation in expenditure we must control for two relatively nonsociological determinants—the sheer number of years welfare programs have existed ("creeping socialism," otherwise known as "incremental budgeting") and the age composition of the population (the more old people, the more pension expenditures). A brief note on each follows.

EDUCATION IS SPECIAL

Despite the collapse of academic standards in some departments and schools in some countries, despite the egalitarian thrust of movements to increase access and reduce tracking by ability in secondary schools, technical institutes, colleges, and universities (see, e.g., Riesman and Grant, 1973), modern education systems remain overwhelmingly meritocratic and vocational, only slightly modified by the counterculture. They admit new masses of students, but at the same time, rather than dropping standards in established curricula, they develop new hierarchies and new specialties—limited arenas of competition at every academic level, which in the end feed appropriate levels of the occupational structure; they diversify to accommodate the immensely varied genetic and cultural advantages and disadvantages of the individuals they process. They loosen up require-

3

ments or abolish traditional grading practices—especially in the
United States—but new incentives emerge, and the general
emphasis on occupationally relevant performance or work habits
remains. Academic credit is given for "life experiences" off
campus, including social and political action or routine jobs, but
that credit is ultimately honored only in the less demanding
niches of the economy—in the shrinking parts of the labor force
where educational entry requirements were and are low. Mean-
while, if academic institutions do not meet elite demands for
technical and administrative personnel and the equally insistent
mass demand for vocational and professional training and
opportunities—and if, like liberal-arts colleges in the United
States, they simultaneously appear politically disruptive—their
budgets are squeezed or they are simply shut down. (In 1968–69,
facing student disruptions which closed Tokyo University, the
conservative government of Japan responded by strengthening
the powers of the Minister of Education to intervene in both
private and public university disputes and to abolish or close
temporarily any university that had not recovered from student
shutdowns. By the end of 1969, after heavy police intervention,
the universities had quieted down. Their budgets continue to be
tightened. Among the reforms recommended by the Central
Commission on Education in 1970 was a proposal to separate
the education and research functions of universities. Michio
Nagai, 1971, pp. 245–258; Burn, 1971, pp. 227–275.)

Why sociologists (Jencks, et al., 1972) should be surprised
that the move from elite to mass to universal education (Trow,
1972) fails to effect by itself a major redistribution of income or
a revolution in equality is a mystery, considering the tight
connection between education and the occupational structure
and the basic sorting and socialization functions of education.
(Durkheim's early remarks about these matters deserve renewed
attention. 1956, pp. 71, 124.)

Related to its accent on admission and tracking criteria
more or less relevant to student performance and occupational
fate, modern higher education is also probably more inegalitar-

ian in its effect on income distribution than any slightly regressive components of health and welfare programs. Although the evidence is in dispute, much of public expenditure on higher education is probably a transfer payment from the parents of the less affluent to the children of the more affluent. The toughest test of this proposition would be the world's largest mass higher-education system, California, where more than eight in ten high-school graduates go on to postsecondary education—the epitome of equality. Comparing average benefits and taxes paid by families with and without children enrolled in the California system in 1964, Hansen and Weisbrod (1969) found that the net outcome was a substantial redistribution upward. Pechman (1970) disputes their findings; he distributes the benefits and costs by income levels and comes to the opposite conclusion that the families with lower incomes received a net subsidy. Looking at the intergenerational transmission of privilege, however, and assessing a great range of data from various communities as well as one national sample, Jencks et al. (1972) estimate that about one-third of the income advantage enjoyed by men from upper-middle-class backgrounds over men from lower-class backgrounds derives from educational advantages: sheer years of extra schooling for those with equal IQs accounts for about 25 percent of the income edge; educational advantages deriving from differences in test scores, for another 10 percent (pp. 215, 216, 346).

✷In none of these studies is the most powerful argument concerning the regressive effects of higher education effectively pursued: namely, that social background affects *quality* of education, which in turn affects lifetime occupational fate. ✦ Because so few mobility studies classify educational institutions by quality, and because fewer still follow the graduates long enough to observe the effect of educational quality on career development, we cannot go beyond plausible argument. From what we know of the subcultures of the highly educated, however, upper-middle-class parents typically transmit their status, income, and influence to their offspring chiefly through

5

an aggressive effort to provide them with a college education superior to that usually given to the middle majority and the poor. In this sustained struggle for protection of privilege across generations, educated parents continue to achieve some success —often against the wishes of their offspring. Whatever the distributional effects of educational subsidies and taxes in California higher education for any one year, there is an unmistakable process of self-selection and recruitment by social background into the three-tier system, with occupational prospects appropriately linked to quality levels. Hundreds of community colleges feed local economies with bank clerks, chefs, supervisors, engineering aides, X-ray technicians, and other semitechnical personnel; the nineteen huge state colleges and universities channel their graduates into more definitely middle-class occupations in teaching, commerce, and industry; while the graduates of the employer-favored campuses of the University of California are typically destined for higher professional and executive positions. (For similar conclusions about the class bias of higher education in Communist countries, see Pryor, 1968, pp. 205–206, 478–481; Rutkevich and Filippov, 1970, pp. 246ff.; and Lipset, 1972.)

A nation's health and welfare effort is clearly and directly a contribution to absolute equality, the reduction of differences between rich and poor, young and old, minority groups and majorities; it is only a secondary contribution to equality of opportunity. In contrast, a nation's educational effort, especially at the higher levels, is chiefly a contribution to equality of opportunity—enhanced mobility for those judged to be potentially able or skilled; it is only a peripheral contribution to absolute equality.

Both in its sources and effects, then, public spending for higher education is different from other parts of the welfare-state package. Thus, for our twenty-two rich countries we expected to find a small negative correlation between social security expenditures and education. The results fit the expectation. For twenty-one countries (data were missing for East

Germany), there is a correlation of −.41 between the best available measure of social security spending for 1966 and the most reliable and comparable indicator of the allocation of resources to education—the percentage of 20–24-year-olds who are in an institution of higher education in 1965 (see Appendix for sample, sources, and measures).[2] As I shall argue below, the ideological underpinnings of the welfare state everywhere reflect a tension between meritocratic and egalitarian values. But the mix varies from program to program, with the meritocratic component for education far more prominent than it is for the rest of the welfare state.

HOUSING BELONGS BUT DATA ARE THIN

The idea that the government should ensure access to decent housing for everyone is widespread in rich countries, although it may be the least fulfilled of welfare-state promises. Housing expenditures are a major component of the standard of living. And, in contrast to education, the structural and ideological roots of public programs to assure a minimum standard of housing are much the same as they are for the rest of the welfare state. Unfortunately, comparable data on public expenditures are as yet available for only a few countries and are, at best, shaky.

A bewildering array of fiscal, monetary, and other policies that affect housing directly and indirectly—even remotely— have made the task of comparative analysis of public spending in this area nearly impossible. When pensions are increased in a national system, one can trace the sources of financing and the

2. For our cross section of sixty-two countries for which we have data on both variables, $r = .53$. Note also table 1, which shows that the enrollment ratio for higher education increases by quartiles of economic growth much as social security spending increases. Compared with the very poor, the richest countries can spend more on everything—for reasons discussed below, pp. 24ff. My argument that social security effort and educational effort are inversely and only loosely related applies only to higher education in rich countries.

7

flow of benefits with little pain. But when government monetary policies lower the interest rate in the mortgage market, thereby creating a boom in construction, and when transportation policies direct rapid transit to a new area, thereby creating a local boom in rents and land values, the idea of "government expenditures for housing" becomes slippery. Consider further the range of government policies directly aimed at changing the housing supply or access to that supply, each with its own price tag and record system. Financial policies include direct loans from public funds, guarantees for loans obtained in the mortgage market or supplements to loans obtained elsewhere, interest-rate subsidies to mortgage associations or banks, rent supplements or housing allowances (related to family or other status and circumstances), and capital grants. Other policies that represent public action or expenditures include construction or management of housing by government and a great assortment of government-stimulated voluntary efforts involving the "backdoor subsidy" of tax relief to owner-occupiers or landlords, co-ops, unions, or other consumer and political groups. To these we must add such public services as roads, main drainage, and sewers, and such public regulations as rent control and code enforcement, with their variable and often unanticipated effects on rents and the stock of housing.

Because the measurement problems are formidable, comparative studies have barely begun; what thin data we have been able to locate suggest the cautious conclusion that government effort and output in this area is moderately correlated with government effort and output in "social security." For the United States and twenty-two countries of Eastern and Western Europe, we obtained the percentage of dwellings completed in 1966 by each of three agencies—public, semipublic, and private investors. Combining the percentages completed by public bodies (states and municipalities or local authorities) and semipublic bodies (housing associations and cooperatives), we found that this figure correlated .36 with the 1966 social security spending of the same countries—consistent with the hypothesis of the coherence of social security and housing.[3] However, students of housing show little confidence in cross-national comparisons for housing; these data are at best suggestive. For the purposes of my study I have been forced to exclude housing until better data become available.

AGE OF SYSTEM AND AGE OF POPULATION AS CONTROLS

If we wish to discover the structural and ideological sources of variation in public spending, we must control for two obvious determinants: the length of time a country has been in the welfare business and the age composition of its population. Austria and Germany, the biggest spenders among the twenty-two richest countries, started sickness and maternity benefits and work-injury insurance in the 1880s; the United States, a

3. Source: United Nations, Economic Commission for Europe, *Annual Bulletin of Housing and Building Statistics for Europe*, V. 13, 1969 (New York, 1970), table 5: "Dwellings completed by type of investor." We excluded dwellings completed by private parties whether aided or unaided by the state. This UN commission provides the best source of European data on housing finance and supply. See also E.C.E. 1968, which reviews housing trends since World War II, and Greve (1971). For the United States the best study is Aaron (1972). Cf. Wendt (1962).

In an earlier exploration of this problem, we constructed a four-item index consisting of two measures of investment ("effort") and two measures of housing quality ("output"). We gave equal weight to each of the four rank orders for eleven European countries as follows: (1) total investment in housing for 1964 as a percent of gross domestic product as reported in the UN Yearbook of *National Accounts Statistics* (1965); (2) per capita investment in housing for 1964 (UN, 1965); (3) number of dwellings per 1,000 inhabitants about 1960; and (4) number of rooms per 1,000 inhabitants about 1960 as reported in a study by the UN Economic Commission for Europe, Vol. 2 (1966). The rank orders combined comprise an index of general housing performance. The index shows a negligible correlation with our rank order of the same countries based on social security expenditures for 1966 ($r_s = .06$). That result, however, is explained by two extreme cases: the country ranked at the top in housing performance, Switzerland, ranks at the bottom in welfare spending; Austria, which ranks low in housing performance, ranks first in welfare spending. Eliminating these two, the correlation for the nine countries becomes positive ($r_s = .62$).

9

welfare-state laggard, did not institute work-injury benefits until about 1911, and only in 1964 moved gingerly toward health insurance with the passage of Medicare. Further, among rich countries, Austria and West Germany were above average in percentage of people at least sixty-five years old in 1966 (Austria, 13.4 percent; West Germany, 12.6 percent); the United States was below average (9.4 percent) (UN *Demographic Yearbook*, 1970).

Students of the welfare state who have put age of system and age of population into quantitative studies have shown that these variables are associated with public spending. For instance, in a multiple regression analysis, Henry Aaron (1967, 1968) found that among twenty-two countries which spend 5 percent or more of their national income on social security, the best predictor of the share of national income spent on social security was the number of decades since the first program was initiated. Time is said to be important for two reasons, both sociologically uninteresting. First, all social-insurance systems "mature." For instance, with no liberalization of benefits or expansion of welfare consciousness, a pension program will become increasingly expensive as more of the covered persons reach retirement age or experience disability or the death of a working spouse. Second, all government budgets are incremental. Once a program is launched, precedent is the major determinant of who gets what the government has to give; and how much goes to the program or agency depends on what it got the last time around (Wildavsky, 1964; cf. Wilensky, 1967, pp. 16ff., 173–191). To make the finding that time counts sociologically useful, however, we must recast it as follows:

The Politics of Bureaucracy. Time will count if a welfare bureaucracy acquires a vested interest in expanding budget and personnel in its area vis-à-vis others, if it successfully cultivates a committed clientele and powerful political allies, and if it effectively spreads information about its benefits and programs. Thus the Austrian welfare bureaucracy, established early, is powerful and self-expanding in the precise sense that it tops other European bureaucracies in size, by the measure of officials per capita. The Austrian bureaucracy further fits the standard pattern of self-aggrandizement; civil service pensions as a fraction of earnings are the highest in Europe, exceeding even the generous German standard.

The success of one agency, however, may mean the relative lag of another. For instance, veterans' benefits in the United States have moved up much faster than unemployment compensation. More important, we cannot assume that all bureaucrats are empire builders. Nor are all agencies imperialistic in aim and entrepreneurial in style. Some bureaucrats seek to defend their professional tasks and integrity, their work routines and general comfort, and their standing with the boss more ardently than they seek to disburse more services and benefits. A top civil servant in Britain, a country that started social security programs early but moved up only slowly, observes: "The long-time bureaucrat in Whitehall—and I've heard this very phrasing—will say, when it is suggested that the program be expanded, shaken up, and generally made more effective and rich, 'We're doing the job; we simply cannot start now mucking about with this or that or the other change. Why, it's clean against the principles of Beveridge'" (interview, 1972).

The Question of Origins and Rates of Growth. To say that they spend a lot because they got there first is to beg two questions: Why do some rich countries start early and others late? How can we explain differential rates of change among both early starters and later starters? To put the weight of explanation on the passage of years is to ignore these basic questions.

Germany, which pioneered the welfare state in the nineteenth century, developed comprehensive programs in all areas except family allowances before 1930 and steadily moved up in spending to arrive today near the top of the list. In contrast, the Netherlands, another welfare-state leader, initiated its health and welfare programs long after Germany, but experienced such swift growth after 1958 as to bring its spending almost up to the German level by 1966 (see table 2 and European Communities, 1972, p. 22). The Netherlands surpassed all Common Market countries by 1970. Time and incremental budgeting cannot explain such extreme differences. Some "socialisms" creep and others gallop.

Age composition in previous studies is generally weaker than program duration as a determinant of aggregate spending for social security. Both Aaron (1967, p. 32; 1968, p. 147) and Pryor (pp. 150, 172, 180) find that the significance of age of population washes out when age of system is included in the same regression. However, with later data and a larger sample than theirs, our results show that for aggregate social security effort (percent of GNP), age of population retains strong predictive power (see fig. 1, p. 25). Further, in analysis of the development of certain programs, age controls may be crucial: the percentage of young (under 15) for education through secondary school and for family or child allowances; the percentage aged 20–24 for higher education; the percentage of old (65 and over) for pensions. Age controls for health insurance are ambiguous (only in the United States are these programs confined to the aged, although the elderly may everywhere use health services and insurance benefits more than the young).

I shall argue below that both program duration and the aging of a population, however powerful, are themselves directly or indirectly a product of economic growth.

CENTRAL SOCIOLOGICAL QUESTIONS

Treating education and the military separately, let us use the phrases "welfare state" or "welfare expenditures and benefits" to describe public consumption expenditures both per capita and as a fraction of GNP (table 1). Further, let us concentrate on the relationship between the welfare state and equality. We can then see that there is very little in social science theory or data to permit firm macro-sociological answers to several key questions:

Determinants

What is the impact of *official ideology and popular sentiment about equality* on the level, types, and administration of welfare expenditures and benefits? Here we deal with the strength of the *urge* for equality.

What is the impact of the *system of government* on the level, types, and administration of welfare expenditures and benefits? Here we deal with the *channels for action* for equality.

How do *levels and rates of economic growth* affect the level, types, and administration of welfare expenditures and benefits? A related and far from trivial question is "What is the impact of *war and military expenditures* on the welfare state?" Here we deal with the economic and political *resources* available to advance equality.

Effects

What is the effect of the welfare state on equality, health, and economic and psychological security? Here we deal with *real welfare outputs*. A related question is "How do the attention and resources devoted to social security affect the capacity to tackle the *newly publicized problems* of pollution and population control, urban decay, and resource exhaustion?"

Flowing from variations in the urge for equality, the channels for action, the resources available, and welfare outputs are variations in the *"welfare backlash."* Is this phenomenon uniquely American, or can we find it in other rich countries where the welfare state is more highly developed and more popular?

The most abstract statement of the sociological problem of the welfare state, then, is this: How do ideology, polity, and economy affect the development of the welfare state, its impact on real welfare, and the political response evoked by both welfare spending and welfare performance?

Few scholars have had the patience to work over existing data or turn up new data that bear directly on these questions. A few researchers have tried: R. M. Titmuss (1958), T. H. Marshall (1965), A. Briggs (1961), G. Myrdal (1960), and G. Rimlinger (1966) among the historical-political writers; P. Cutright (1965), M. Gordon (1963), H. Aaron (1967), W. Galenson (1968), F. L.

13

Pryor (1968), K. Taira and P. Kilby (1969), and B. M. Russett (1970) among the students using more quantitative and comparative economic data. They have found more questions than answers, more gaps in the evidence than data. The first aim of my current study is to specify some of those gaps and point to significant research questions implied by the work of these scholars and by my own work. The second aim is to test hypotheses about the relative importance of economic, political, and cultural determinants of welfare-state development. The third aim is to explore the effect of all these expenditures on real welfare—explore, because many necessary indicators of the quality of life are not yet available across many nations in sufficiently comparable form. Chapters 2, 3, and 4 will (1) review evidence bearing on the macro-sociological problems, concentrating on a cross section of sixty-four countries, and (2) specify more concrete hypotheses that help explain the origin and divergent development of the welfare state among the twenty-two richest countries. Chapter 5 explores the toughest problem —the effects of all this spending on real welfare.

2

Economic Level, Ideology, and Social Structure

While there is general agreement that the main explanation for welfare-state development is economic development and its universal social and political correlates (see Wilensky and Lebeaux, 1958, p. 230), there is considerable uncertainty about the relative weight of level of economic growth, ideology or cultural values and beliefs (collectivistic and individualistic, egalitarian and less egalitarian), and social structure (economic system, political system) as determinants of the level, types, and administration of welfare expenditures and benefits.

LEVEL OF ECONOMIC GROWTH

In the past century the welfare state has developed in every urban-industrial country. Although they vary greatly in civil liberties and civil rights, the rich countries vary little in their general strategy for constructing the floor below which no one sinks. The values invoked to defend the welfare state—social justice, political order, efficiency, or equality—depend on the group articulating the defense. But the action in the end has produced one of the major structural uniformities of modern societies. The richer countries become, the more likely they are to broaden the coverage of both population and risks—that is, they will insure more people against seven or eight risks of modern life: risks of injury on the job, sickness or maternity or both, old age, invalidism and death, reduced standard of living because of increased family size (offset by family allowances), and unemployment. However reluctant the government or the more affluent citizens may be, they are moved toward the welfare state by needs for political order (under conditions of the push for equality) and stable economic incentives.

The best evidence for the dominance of economic levels in social security development has been presented by Cutright (1965), Aaron (1967), and Pryor (1968). As indexes of "level of social and economic development," Cutright relies on energy consumption, urbanization, and literacy; as a clue to welfare-state development, he relies on an index of "social insurance program experience" (the number of years a nation has had any of five Guttman-scaled programs in operation—work injury, sickness and/or maternity, old age, invalidism and death, family allowance, unemployment insurance). He shows that among seventy-six nations social security coverage most powerfully correlates with level of economic development. However, Cutright gives no attention to changes in levels of *expenditure* or to measures of ability to pay other than energy consumption (e.g., to GNP).

In multiple regression analyses using different measures and controlling for age of the system, other students have also found affluence associated with social security development, but their results are more ambiguous. Aaron (1967) uses per capita national income, per capita social security expenditures, and social security expenditures as a percentage of national income in twenty-two countries for 1957. He finds that per capita income, alone and with other variables, is the most important determinant of per capita social security outlays, even superior to age of system, but is insignificant as a determinant of the percentage of national income spent on social security. That finding held for a replication on 1960 data (Pechman, Aaron, and Taussig, 1968, pp. 295–296).[1] In the most thorough cross-national study of public consumption expenditures in the literature, Pryor (1968) compares seven "communist" and seven "capitalist" countries, deriving his own estimates of GNP and public spending from published and unpublished data, including national budget documents in the relevant languages and the work of relevant ministries, statistical offices, and scholars, checked by interviews in finance ministries and similar agencies. He finds that system age is the most important predictor of health and welfare spending, and he confirms the ambiguous role of economic level. In his cross-sectional analysis, per capita GNP is not related to the share of GNP going to public consumption expenditures for health or welfare or education, but in his time-series analysis economic level is important for all three ratios (pp. 179, 180, 205, 219).

These somewhat divergent conclusions about the importance of economic level in welfare-state development can be explained by differences in samples and by the usual differences in cross-section and time-series data. The greater the range of riches and spending brought to view for any one year, the more important economic level will be. Compare Cutright's seventy-

1. In my study I concentrate on percent of GNP as a rough measure of welfare *effort*—the budget decisions of political elites as they allocate scarce resources among competing ends. Social security expenditures per head of recipient population, in contrast, is a rough measure of welfare *output*, which I am analyzing separately and do not report here. When 1966 per capita income among the twenty-two "rich" countries in my tables 2 and 4 varies by a factor of about 4 (Japan $952, U.S. $3,542), the per capita expenditures for social security will naturally be somewhat different from the social security share of GNP. A big effort by the least affluent countries to cover everyone will spread benefits thin; a small effort by a very rich country to do the same will make the per capita expenditure quite high. Thus by the measure of per capita expenditures two of the five richest countries in table 2 (Canada and the U.S.) move up to the middle, while two of the four poorest countries (Austria and Italy) move from top to bottom. What is striking, however, is the relative stability of the other leaders and laggards, whichever measure we use. Sweden, already high, moves up to a class of its own—tops by every measure we can devise. (Cf. McGranahan, 1970, p. 51.)

six non-African countries which had achieved independence by
1960 with Aaron's more homogeneous sample of countries
which spend at least 5 percent of GNP on social security, and
with Pryor's fourteen countries—seven centrally planned, paired
with seven market economies of roughly equal wealth or, in the
case of the United States versus the USSR, power. The second
source of variation in findings is simply the process of social
change. Time-series data capture shifts in demographic structure, ideology, technology, and social organization; cross-
sectional data do not—although, if the range of comparison is
wide, one can infer these changes.

Table 1 reports 1966 data consistent with Cutright's
finding; it affirms the importance of level of economic growth as
a source of social security spending for sixty-four countries at
four levels of per capita income. Both this table and Pryor's
analysis of time series (1968, pp. 181, 290) are consistent with
Wilensky's hypothesis (1965, p. x) of a slowdown in the rate of
increase in social security spending. Note that the average ratio
of social security to GNP for the richest sixteen countries is only
slightly higher than that for the next sixteen. As rich countries
become richer, they may enter a stage of affluence when the
population can buy so much on the market or bargain for so
much privately, and when the resistance to welfare spending
hardens so much that the percentage of GNP spent on the
welfare state will creep up only slowly, level off, or even drop. I
shall explore the sources of resistance to welfare spending in
chapter 3.

ECONOMIC AND POLITICAL SYSTEMS

The best evidence that modern societies converge appears in
data showing that political system is a weak predictor of major
components of public consumption spending and that economic
system is irrelevant. Pryor's careful comparison of market and
centralized economies demonstrates that when factors other
than economic system are held constant, his seven communist

TABLE 1: *Quartile Averages of Social Security Spending and Military Spending as a Percent of GNP, 1966 or Nearest Year, and Enrollment Ratios for Total Population 20–24 in Higher Education, 1965 or Nearest Year, for 64 Countries Ranked by Per Capita GNP*

		Quartile averages		
Quartiles of 64 countries ranked on per capita GNP at factor cost, 1966[a]	*Per capita GNP in U.S. dollars, 1966*	*Social security spending as percent of GNP, 1966 or nearest year*[b]	*Military spending as percent of GNP, 1966 or nearest year*[c]	*Enrollment ratios for total population 20–24 in higher education (total no. enrolled/ total no. 20–24), nearest year*[d]
First quartile (richest 16 nations)—U.S. through the Netherlands	$2,073	13.8	3.8	13.5
Second quartile— Czechoslovakia through Greece	$ 948	10.1	4.5	12.0
Third quartile— Cyprus through El Salvador	$ 372	4.0	2.8	4.1
Fourth quartile (poorest 16 nations)—Ghana through Upper Volta	$ 156	2.5	4.0	2.1

[a] All countries for which data on social security spending, military spending, and GNP at factor cost were available for 1966.

TABLE 1 *(continued)*

ᵇ The source for social security expenditure data for all countries except East Germany was the ILO, *The Cost of Social Security, 1964–1966* (Geneva: 1972), pp. 317–323. East German data are from the Bundesministerium für innerdeutsche Beziehungen, *Bericht des Bundesregierung und Materialien zur Lage der Nation, 1971* (Bonn: 1971), p. 397.

ᶜ The source for military expenditure data for all countries except the USSR, Australia, and New Zealand was the U.S. Arms Control and Disarmament Agency, *World Military Expenditures, 1971* (Washington: 1972), pp. 18–21. For the USSR, the source of military data was the Institute for Strategic Studies, *The Military Balance, 1972–1973* (London: 1973), p. 73. For Australia and New Zealand, the source used was the Stockholm International Peace Research Institute, *SIPRI Yearbook of World Armaments and Disarmaments, 1969/70* (Uppsala: 1970), pp. 274–276.

ᵈ UNESCO, *Statistical Yearbook, 1971* (Louvain, Belgium: UNESCO, 1972), table 2.7, pp. 101–119.

and seven capitalist countries are indistinguishable by their public expenditures for health and welfare and converge between 1956 and 1962 in their spending for education (1968, pp. 282–285). Expenditures converge even for "internal security"— police, courts, and prisons—although if traffic control expenditures are removed, communist countries retain a clear edge in their devotion to internal security through surveillance and terror (Pryor, 1968, pp. 180, 205, 248). On items with a big price tag, except for internal security, economic system does not count.

The weakness of political system as an explanation of welfare-state development is best demonstrated by Cutright, who shows that economic level is far more important as a predictor of social security coverage than his index of "political representativeness," although representative governments do introduce welfare programs earlier than less representative governments at the same "energy" level.

To explore the effect of gross differences in political system vis-à-vis economic level, age of social security system, and demographic structure, we devised a typology of political systems, a modification of Blondel's classification of the polities of the world circa 1968. His scheme classifies countries according to three continua: economic "ideology" (left, center, right), extent of democracy, and extent of coerciveness of the state (Blondel, 1969, pp. 37–42, 111–116, 531–546). Because we have more distinct measures of economic ideology, and because Blondel's actual grouping of countries is a reflection less of political norms and economic ideology than of the structural arrangements for popular participation and civil liberties, we used these structural criteria to classify our sixty-four countries. The criteria were (1) the degree to which the mass of citizens participate in decision making, a continuum from populist to oligarchical; and (2) the degree to which the state allows or encourages the voluntary action of numerous autonomous groups, a continuum that ranges from liberal-democratic polities, in which institutionalized opposition and the concomitant civil liberties flourish, to totalitarian polities, in which institutionalized opposition and associated civil liberties are eliminated. These two dimensions yield four types of political systems in which we classified our sixty-four countries: "liberal democratic" (U.K., Sweden), "authoritarian populist" (Mexico, Syria), "authoritarian oligarchic" (Spain, Portugal), or "totalitarian" (USSR, East Germany) (cf. Linz, 1964).[2] These types, of course, miss the nuance that can distinguish the limited cultural freedom of Yugoslavia or Poland from the repression of the USSR or East Germany or, for that matter, the variable use of terror over the life of one regime. Similarly, they obscure the different levels of popular participation in such Western countries as the United States, with its relatively low voter turnout, and the Netherlands, where virtually the entire electorate shows up at the polls. But the classification suffices for my purpose.

2. High mass participation and low coerciveness—liberal democracies; high mass participation and high coerciveness—totalitarian; medium to high participation and medium coerciveness—authoritarian populist; low participation and medium to high coerciveness—authoritarian oligarchic. Table 8 in the Appendix lists countries by political system. Four countries were eliminated from this analysis because of missing data on proportion of persons 65+ in the population.

The zero-order correlations between social security effort on the one hand, and age of the social security system, fraction of aged in the total population, per capita GNP, and political system on the other hand, are presented in table 5 (Appendix). All data center on the year 1966. If my theory about the primacy of economic level and its demographic and bureaucratic correlates is correct, the correlations between social security spending, economic level, age of system, and age of population should be strong, while the correlations between social security effort and military effort, or social security effort and political system should be weak. The results generally follow this pattern. Social security spending as a fraction of GNP is most strongly correlated with population age (.89), log_e of age of system (.85), and per capita GNP (.67). The lesser correlations of social security effort with each political system type (liberal democracy, .45; oligarchic authoritarian, −.47; and populist authoritarian, −.33) are spuriously high; liberal-democratic countries tend to be rich ($r = .55$) and rich countries tend to spend more on social security; conversely, the authoritarian systems tend to be poor and poor countries spend little on social security. Totalitarian systems have more variance in per capita GNP, so they constitute an ambiguous case. There is no significant correlation between military effort and social security effort for this sixty-country cross section.

If we include each of these four types of political systems as dummy variables in a path diagram (see fig. 1) we find that each of the two "cleanest" categories—liberal democracy and totalitarianism—contributes only a little to the explanation of social security effort; the two authoritarian types contribute almost nothing and are eliminated from the diagram.[3]

3. For an explanation of path analysis, see Land, 1969; Heise, 1969; and Duncan, 1966. Paths and path coefficients in figure 1 were arrived at in two stages. In the first stage, the following three regressions were run. Social security effort was regressed on all variables shown in the correlation matrix "Simple Correlates of Social Security Spending," Appendix, table 5; then age of social security system (log_e) was regressed on all variables except social security effort; then percent of

The path diagram below unscrambles the significant causes of social security effort in a model that makes the best theoretical sense. It is based on a multiple regression described by the following three equations:

$$X_6 = p_{61}X_1 + p_{62}X_2 + p_{63}X_3 + p_{64}X_4 + p_{65}X_5 + p_{6w}R_w.$$
$$X_5 = p_{51}X_1 + p_{52}X_2 + p_{53}X_3 + p_{54}X_4 + p_{5v}R_v.$$
$$X_4 = p_{41}X_1 + p_{42}X_2 + p_{43}X_3 + p_{4u}R_u.$$

where

X_6 is social security effort measured by social security/GNP in 1966;

---

persons sixty-five and older in the population was regressed on all variables except social security effort and age of social security system ($\log_e$). Certain variables, such as military spending, as predicted, had *no* statistically significant relationships in *any* of the regressions; they were dropped from the analysis. Where statistically significant relationships existed (p $<$.05), direct paths were drawn to show them; where no significant relationship emerged in the regression, no path appears.

In the second stage, the three regressions above were run again, using only those variables that had produced at least one significant relationship. The path coefficients in figure 1 are the standardized partial regression coefficients (also called beta weights or path coefficients, and denoted by the letter p) that appeared in this second run. The path coefficients for the second stage are slightly different from the corresponding coefficients in the first stage, since statistically insignificant variables are omitted in the second stage.

This two-stage procedure also produced the paths and path coefficients of figures 2 and 3. However, because of their special theoretical relevance, the nonsignificant paths of the first stage are illustrated by dotted lines in those two diagrams. Indicating their weakness as causal determinants, the path coefficients above the dotted lines are generally much smaller than those above solid lines. The path coefficients above the solid lines were obtained, as before, by running the regressions a second time, after omitting the nonsignificant (dotted-line) variables.

Indirect influences of independent variables are indicated by multiplying the path coefficients of all paths leading ultimately to the dependent variable. In the text discussing figure 1 such indirect effects are designated by subscripts such as the following ($p_{64}p_{41} = .32$), where the path coefficient from social security effort (X_6) to age of population (X_4), .52, is multiplied by the path from age of population (X_4) to GNP per capita (X_1), .62, to yield .32, the strength of the indirect influence of GNP per capita on social security effort via the aged as a fraction of the population.

X_5 is the age of the system through 1966 measured by the natural logarithm of the sum of the years of operation of each of five social security programs;

X_4 is the percentage of people aged sixty-five years and over in the total population in 1966;

X_3 is a dummy variable, the presence or absence of a totalitarian state about 1966;

X_2 is a dummy variable, the presence or absence of a liberal democratic state about 1966;

X_1 is economic level measured by GNP per capita in 1966;

R_w, R_v, and R_u are residuals,

and all six variables are expressed in standardized form.

This entire model accounts for 83 percent of the variance in social security effort, 74 percent of the variance in age of system, and 61 percent of the variance in age of population.

Although economic level and social security effort are strongly correlated ($r = .67$), the path diagram, figure 1, shows that this relationship is largely mediated first through the proportion of aged in the population ($p_{64}p_{41} = .32$) and, second, through both age of population and age of system ($p_{65}p_{54}p_{41} = .16$). This confirms previous theories that economic growth is the ultimate cause of welfare-state development (Wilensky and Lebeaux, 1958, p. 230) and at the same time underscores two powerful intervening processes.

It has been shown repeatedly that social security programs simply do not appear without sufficient national surplus to make them a policy option, or if, as in many poor countries these programs are enacted, they remain weak paper programs or are severely restricted in coverage until such surplus is produced. For instance, Cutright (1965), as we have seen, demonstrates that economic level is the main determinant of the number of years of social-insurance program experience. But he leaves out what our path diagram shows to be the strongest direct cause of both program experience and social security effort—the fraction of aged. In figure 1, the two strongest direct paths are the direct

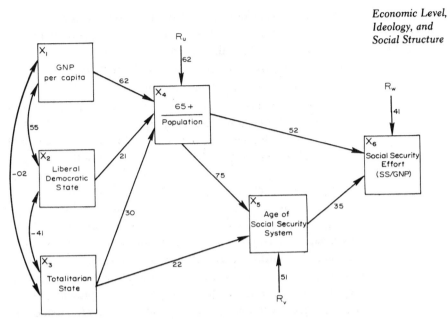

FIGURE 1. Causal Model of Social Security Spending: 60 Countries.
Solid lines indicate relationships with p < .05; nonsignificant paths
have been omitted.

flow from the aged to social security spending (p_{64} = .52) and
the direct flow from age of system to spending (p_{65} = .35).

I have already indicated why the countries with older
systems spend more of their resources on social security—all
systems mature and all government budgets are incremental. As
the years roll by, more of the covered persons either reach
retirement age or experience disability or the death of a working
spouse; the mass of citizens press for higher benefits and
expanded coverage for themselves and their dependent relatives;
political elites see a greater need for programs; bureaucrats
entrench, cultivate budget, personnel, and clientele; while
politicians, bureaucrats, and the mass alike spread information
about the programs, thereby encouraging claims and reinforcing
the demand for more.

A high proportion of aged is more complexly rooted in

25

economic growth. Considering a cross section with a great range of per capita income or a lengthy time series, economic growth has produced a marked decline in birthrates, which is the main reason so many rich countries have a high percentage of the aged. Leaving migration aside and assuming that death rates do not increase, every day the birthrate declines the proportion of people aged sixty-five and over creeps up. If we concentrate only on the small number of rich countries, we find some variation in this historical drop in birthrates and the concomitant aging of the population. For instance, the birthrates of European countries and Japan have moved down faster and further—and moved up less in the baby boom that followed World War II—than have the birthrates of the United States, Canada, Australia, and New Zealand. But when we compare large numbers of countries representing a great range of wealth, as in our sample of sixty, we find that big differences in past trends in birthrates have produced sharp contrasts in the present proportion of aged by level of economic development. Hence the strong correlation between economic level and the percentage of those aged sixty-five and over $(r = .89)$ and the strong path from GNP per capita to percentage of aged $(p_{41} = .62)$.

Old people under modern conditions will, of course, constitute a population in need and a political force for further social security development. Hence the strong correlations between age of population, years of program operation, and spending. The aged are the main current beneficiaries of the two most expensive programs—pensions and health insurance. They are also a prime beneficiary of public assistance or social assistance. The political pressure for expansion of these programs, however, is only partly their own "gray power." For if we did not have pension, health, and welfare payments, many beneficiaries would be partly or wholly supported by relatives or others—self-supporting persons who would otherwise be forced to share their income with present beneficiaries (Gordon, 1963, p. 25, and Wilensky, 1965, pp. xiii-xiv). This possibility is perhaps a major political appeal for social security expansion:

shift the burden either of guilt or of financial responsibility from the children of aging, sick parents to the government by means of a small social security tax. Such an appeal was surely a factor in the passage of Medicare for the aged in the United States, whose government resisted any national health plan long after every other rich country had embraced the idea. Finally, insofar as urban affluence undermines the economic value of children and increases anxiety among those middle-aged citizens who think about their own security in old age, the entire adult population exerts pressure for programs geared to the needs of the aged.

For all these reasons, we find strong correlations between age of population, years of program operation, and spending. That the welfare state is fundamentally focused on the aged is reflected in the strong path coefficients of figure 1. We can infer the following process from these cross-sectional data of 1966: As economic level climbs, the percentage of aged climbs, which shapes spending directly; with economic growth the percentage of aged goes up, which makes for an early start and swift spread of social security programs (reflected in our index of age of system), which, in turn, is expressed in big spending. In fact, used singly or jointly, these two "control" variables—processes intervening between economic level and social security effort—account for at least 75 percent of the variance in social security spending in any multiple regression they enter.

For this sixty-country sample, the primacy of economic level and its demographic and bureaucratic correlates is support for a convergence hypothesis; economic growth makes countries with contrasting cultural and political traditions more alike in their strategy for constructing the floor below which no one sinks. Further evidence of convergence of rich countries is the finding that authoritarian polities have no significant effects net of economic level, while the other two types of political systems, liberal democracy and totalitarianism, have only a small independent influence on social security effort. And insofar as they count, the two systems work in the same direction—increased welfare effort. Incidentally, the path diagram (fig. 1) shows that the small influence of the two political types is entirely indirect; liberal democracy makes its contribution through age of population and age of system and through its correlation with GNP; totalitarianism makes its contribution through age of population and age of system.[4]

This is not to say that political arrangements are irrelevant to welfare-state development. As I shall argue below, for rich countries a major political variable explaining contrasts in welfare effort is the degree of centralization of government, a political fact that varies so greatly within the category "liberal democracy" that the customary contrast between pluralist and totalitarian explains little.

IDEOLOGY AND THE WELFARE BACKLASH:
AN AMERICAN PECULIARITY?

Whatever the economic system (reliance on direct controls versus reliance on indirect controls and market mechanisms), and whatever the political system (pluralist, authoritarian, totalitarian), the rich countries develop a common social-insurance strategy. Despite their similar programs and expanding coverage, however, these countries vary in the fraction of their public resources spent on health and welfare and in the level and organization of benefits and services. The differences among rich countries in table 2 are not trivial. Consider the spread in percentage of GNP devoted to social security in pairs of countries roughly matched for economic level: Sweden's 17.5

---

4. A stepwise regression of percentage of aged on level of economic develop-ment and the two political types yields the following results:

Dependent Variable	Independent Variable	Variance Explained (R^2)
65+/population	Per capita GNP	.54
65+/population	Per capita GNP + totalitarian state	.59
65+/population	Per capita GNP + totalitarian state + liberal-democratic state	.61

versus Switzerland's 9.5; West Germany's 19.6 versus the United States' 7.9; Czechoslovakia's 17.2 versus the USSR's 10.1; Austria's whopping 21.0 versus Japan's lean 6.2. Such variations demand explanation going beyond economic growth, demographic structure, the age of the system, and political and economic system.

One loose but popular explanation invokes national differences in values and beliefs. Do terms like "collectivistic" versus "individualistic," "egalitarian" versus "less egalitarian," or even "communist" versus "noncommunist" permit us to classify countries by welfare-state development? If so, what are the structural props for pro-welfare-state and anti-welfare-state doctrines? In what populations and institutions are egalitarian values anchored? How do they relate to other values rooted in other structural facts?

I begin with the assumption that there is no reason to expect welfare-state ideologies to be consistent with other equally strong, also universal values. For the values of equality and humanitarianism that sustain the welfare state are in conflict with the free mobility ideology and the commitment to economic growth that *also* characterize rich countries. With an eye to internal comparisons of the beliefs of "modern" and "less modern" populations within one country, as well as cross-national comparison, I shall first consider "economic individualism" and the welfare backlash, and then "economic collectivism" and other sentiments supporting the welfare state. I shall argue that these values and beliefs everywhere appear side by side.

I shall also present data on up to twenty-two countries for which we could measure various aspects of elite ideology—an index of belief in "planning for equality" (twenty-two countries) and an unrelated indicator of belief in "equal opportunity" (fourteen countries). These data show not only that, as a source of welfare effort, economic level is more important than political system, but also that together they overwhelm elite ideology.

TABLE 2: *Recent Trends in Social Security Spending as a Percent of GNP at Factor Cost for 22 Countries*

Country[a]	1966	1949	1952	1955	1958	1961	1964	1965	1966	1967	1968	1969	1970
Austria	21.0	11.6	17.7	16.5	18.5	19.0	20.2	20.5	21.0				
Germany (FR)	19.6	13.7	17.0	17.4	20.5	18.0	18.6	19.0	19.6	23.3	23.1	22.9	22.6
Belgium	18.5	11.8	13.2	14.2	15.9	17.0	16.2	17.9	18.5	19.4	20.2	20.1	19.5
Netherlands	18.3	8.1	9.4	9.2	10.8	12.2	15.6	16.9	18.3	20.1	21.6	22.0	23.0
France	18.3	11.0	15.2	16.0	16.3	16.1	17.8	18.3	18.3	21.5	21.4	21.2	20.9
Sweden	17.5	9.1	9.7	11.6	12.8	12.9	15.6	16.3	17.5				
Italy	17.5	8.2	10.2	11.2	12.8	12.8	14.4	16.5	17.5	20.0	21.1	21.1	21.1
Czechoslovakia	17.2	...	11.9	14.3	15.2	15.8	17.3	17.3	17.2				
East Germany	16.4	...	...	...	...	...	...	16.7	16.4	16.5	17.1		
United Kingdom	14.4	10.6	11.4	10.9	12.1	12.6	13.2	14.1	14.4				
Denmark	13.9	7.8	9.8	10.5	12.5	11.0	12.7	12.5	13.9				
Finland	13.1	6.2	8.6	8.4	10.6	10.3	11.1	11.9	13.1				
Norway	12.6	6.5	6.9	8.3	10.0	10.6	12.2	12.4	12.6				
New Zealand	11.8	9.5	10.8	10.6	11.1	12.9	11.3	11.4	11.8				
Ireland	11.1	7.2	7.9	9.7	11.1	9.8	9.9	10.6	11.1				
USSR	10.1	...	...	8.1	10.2	9.6	9.0	9.8	10.1				
Canada	10.1	6.1	6.1	8.2	8.9	10.2	10.6	10.7	10.1				

Switzerland	9.5	5.8	6.7	7.2	8.3	8.3	9.2	9.2	9.5
Australia	9.0	4.3	6.5	7.3	8.3	9.2	8.9	8.9	9.0
Israel	8.0	3.9	5.8	6.2	7.5	7.2	6.9	7.7	8.3
United States	7.9	4.4	4.7	5.4	6.8	7.7	7.9	7.7	7.9
Japan	6.2	....	4.2	5.3	5.3	4.7	5.5	6.0	6.2

[a] The source for social security spending figures for all nations 1949–66, except East Germany, is the ILO, *The Cost of Social Security, 1964–1966* (Geneva: 1972), pp. 317–323. For East Germany, the source of data for all years is the Bundesministerium für innerdeutsche Beziehungen, *Bericht des Bundesregierung und Materialien zur Lage der Nation 1971* (Bonn: 1971), p. 397. The source of data for the Common Market countries, 1967–70, is the European Communities Statistical Office, *Sozialkonten, 1962–1970* (Luxembourg: 1972), pp. 18–19. Factor cost GNP is used instead of market price GNP to make more valid comparisons of countries that vary in their reliance on indirect taxes. See Appendix on Methods for definitions and explanations.

[b] Year or nearest year. In some cases, fiscal years were the only years for which data on social security spending were available. Thus, data for fiscal year 1949–50 were used for 1949, 1952–53 for 1952, and so forth.

Economic Individualism. Although the demands of modern technology impose no rigid mold on a culture, all modern societies face similar problems, and their solutions to these problems are similar. For instance, every industrial system requires some competition for occupational position on the basis of criteria relevant to the performance of the role, as well as some system of special reward for the development of scarce talents and skills. It is plausible to assume that these universal structural features of modern economies foster similar mobility ideologies, that in the most diverse political and cultural contexts doctrines of economic individualism take root: increasing portions of the population in modernizing sectors believe that everyone has an equal opportunity to achieve a better job, that everyone has the moral duty to make the most of his talents, to try to get ahead, that if a person fails it is at least partly his own fault, and so on. Such notions are widespread in the United States, and I have not found evidence that they are confined to its least modern sectors; nor can we assume that the success ideology is absent in countries where the welfare state is more popular (Wilensky, 1966, p. 103; and Wilensky and Lebeaux, 1958, pp. 40–48). Without proper comparison, an intensive look at the welfare scene in the United States blinds one's vision of these wider ideological similarities.

It is true that the United States is more reluctant than almost any other rich country to make a welfare effort appropriate to its affluence. Our support of national welfare programs is halting; our administration of services for the less privileged is mean. We move toward the welfare state, but we do it with ill grace, carping and complaining all the way (Wilensky, 1965, pp.xvii ff.; Wilensky and Lebeaux, 1958, pp. 33–48). It is tempting to attribute this reluctance to cultural values—our economic individualism, our unusual emphasis on private property, the free market, and minimum government—because they permeate so many areas of American life.

For instance, these values are reflected in the welfare backlash of the past decade—the urge to punish the poor for their poverty. In 1961 Newburgh, New York, became a symbol of the attack on welfare services as the cry of "welfare scandal" went out across the land; welfare recipients were faced with a choice between police interrogation and fingerprinting or the loss of benefits (Ritz, 1966, pp. 36–40). Most striking was the prominence of welfare issues in California politics from 1966 to 1973. In the California gubernatorial race of 1966, Hollywood actor Ronald Reagan almost brought down the house when he asserted that welfare recipients are on "a prepaid lifetime vacation plan." In 1970, after four years in office, with taxes rising, welfare costs soaring, and campus disruption recurring (all of which he had vowed to stop), Governor Reagan ran and won on the same slogans: "We are fighting the big spending politicians who advocate a welfare state, the welfare bureaucrats whose jobs depend on expanding the welfare system and the cadres of professional poor who have adopted welfare as a way of life" (*Wall Street Journal*, October 9, 1970). For political advantage the slogan "welfare chiseling" was in 1966 second only to the slogan "get Berkeley." By 1970 the welfare issue had moved to top place, where it remained in the ideological politics of California through the early seventies.

New York, California—these are rich states, not poor ones, and it is here in the vanguard of affluence that both taxes and welfare costs climb fastest relative to the generally low taxes and welfare benefits of the United States. For instance, the four states with the steepest rise in the caseload for Aid to Families with Dependent Children from 1960 to 1969 are New York (up 271 percent), Maryland, Massachusetts, and California (up 219 percent) (Piven and Cloward, 1971, Appendix, table 1). The tax take in such states is also well above the relatively low U.S. average of 28 percent in 1966. The estimated fraction of "gross state product" paid in taxes by residents of New York was 36 percent in 1965–66; Californians paid 34 percent. That puts New York above the United Kingdom, and California even with Denmark. (Estimates derived from OECD, *National Accounts Statistics*, as of 1966; Pechman, 1971, p. 287; and Maxwell, 1969,

33

pp. 249–252.) And it is in these rich states, too, that the comfortable majority believe that people on relief, people without jobs, are lazing comfortably on the dole or on unemployment compensation.

That the ideology of economic individualism is widespread in modern sectors of the United States is further evident in survey data which, although they seldom deal directly with welfare issues, are good indirect clues. First, there is the consistent finding that dominant, growing upper and middle strata articulate that ideology. From Hyman (1953) to Rytina, Form, and Pease (1970), surveys have shown that adherence to the free mobility ideology is greatest among those who profit most from the reiteration of the ideology. But what is crucial is not the differences between white and black, rich and poor, but the absolute *level* of support for the success ideology *throughout* the system—overwhelming support among the upper two-thirds or so of the American population and, more striking, among large fractions of the very poorest and most deprived populations, who go along with the dominant optimistic majority.[5]

Finally, the success ideology appears in countries where the

5. Rytina, Form, and Pease, like other students of stratification, are impressed by the differences, but their tables, p. 709, typically show that almost a majority of the lowest and middle strata share the views of the well off. Cf. Form and Huber (1971, p. 679), where in a Muskegon, Michigan, sample in which about half of everyone agreed that "people on relief are lazy," 28 percent of poor blacks and 36 percent of middle-income blacks also agreed. G. Marx (1967, p. 24) reports that in 1964 about two-thirds of a national cross section of blacks agreed with the statement "Negroes who want to work hard can get ahead just as easily as anyone else"—a distribution of opinion almost the same as that for whites in the same survey (Selznick and Steinberg, 1969, p. 171). Two surveys in Baltimore uncover a similar pattern: a sample of black working-class students were less likely than their middle-class peers to believe that there are barriers to equal opportunity (Simmons and Rosenberg, 1971, pp. 235–249); and a sample of adult black women living in Baltimore in 1964 evidenced negligible differences from white women in their response to such assertions as "There are too many people receiving welfare who should be working" (78 percent of blacks agree; 81 percent of whites), and "Too many women receiving ADC are having illegitimate babies in order to increase the amount of money they get" (48 percent of blacks agree; 50 percent of whites) (Kallen and Miller, 1971).

welfare state is more popular, too. Systematic, reliable surveys comparing two or more countries on any topic are very rare, and surveys tapping these ideological themes even rarer. But we have a few indirect clues from a 1968 survey of aspirations and consumer behavior in the Netherlands, Britain, Germany, and the United States by Katona, Strumpel, and Zahn (1971). Although this is one of the best cross-national surveys, it presents a rather sketchy treatment of age, education, and income as determinants of mobility orientation and the desire to work and consume. Nevertheless, the data generally suggest that vanguard populations in Europe—the young and educated—display the same optimism relative to older people that they do in the United States and, by loose inference, more adherence to the success ideology, too. Compared with more established older people, they are optimistic about their future income and well-being, more eager to work, more enthusiastic consumers who buy more and plan to buy still more luxury goods (pp. 65ff., 72, 134).[6] They are like the "Happy Good Citizen-Consumers" I uncovered in a 1960 American survey (Wilensky, 1964, pp.

6. The chain of reasoning from their findings must be indirect. The percentage of family heads under 35 who expect to be better off in four years is much greater in all countries than the percentage of optimistic family heads over 50 or 55 (p. 205):

	Younger	Older
U.S.	79	13
England	66	12
Germany	46	11
Holland	43	10

In a multiple-classification analysis explaining these optimistic expectations, age is much more strongly related to expectations (beta coefficient .44) than is income (.11) or past economic gains (.15). (Table A-6, p. 209.) Inflation, surprisingly, does not greatly affect group and national differences in optimism (p. 53). At the time of this survey, for instance, Britain was fresh from the shock of devaluation and yet remained closer to American optimism than to Continental skepticism (p. 179). It may take a crisis as deep as the energy crunch of 1974 to dampen drastically such consumer optimism. The relevant findings on consumer aspirations and eagerness to work are on pp. 72, 130, 216, 219, 221–222. Regarding education, the authors assert (p. 57) that the perception of cumulative gains increases with educational level in all four countries, but they present only sketchy data (p. 206).

195–196). Katona, Strumpel, and Zahn believe that the average American gives himself more individual credit for past success than the average Dutchman, Englishman, or German. Unfortunately, they report relevant data only for the United States; apparently interviewing was neither comparable nor thorough for the other countries on this issue.[7]

Because of elite education systems in Europe, the educated young are a smaller fraction of the total than they are in the United States and do not yet set mass styles of life. Also they are not as optimistic-enthusaistic as young educated Americans. However, as postsecondary education spreads in Holland, Britain, and Germany, the vanguard mobility aspirations apparent among the young, which I infer from the four-country survey, may become mass aspirations, and the gap between the United States and Europe will close.[8]

In short, a universal elite requirement for incentives fosters mass adherence to a success ideology, one source of the welfare backlash among modern segments of every rich country.

Economic Collectivism.   A similar elite demand for incentives underlies pro-welfare-state doctrines—not incentives to make

7. Of the American household heads who perceive that they are better off than four years ago, 42 percent attribute that success to their own efforts (p. 56). The question was open-ended, the interview conversational.

8. One clue in Katona, Strumpel, and Zahn supports this convergence view: Britain's labor force averages 9.7 years of formal education, the highest in Western Europe; Britain also leads in percentage of college students of working-class background (OECD, 1971, p. 56), although in 1966 it was about even with West Germany and behind Holland in percent of 20–24-year-olds in postsecondary education. Consistent with the expectation of ideological convergence rooted in educational opportunity, the British were closest to the Americans in their optimistic assessments of their past and expected financial situation (p. 179). I am assuming that the worldwide spread of the counterculture—however influential in dress, speech, music, and interstitial styles of life—is peripheral to the economic structure and marginal to the growing professional-technical-vocational institutions that feed that structure. See pp. 3–7 above and my comments in Rositi, ed. (1973), Vol. 3, pp. 322–325. For clues to similar ideological effects of education in the Soviet Union, see Lipset (1972), pp. 99–101.

36

the most talented use their talents, train for the most complex jobs, and so on, but incentives to keep the least successful in the race, or at least working. As Bismarck foresaw, a pension at the end of a life of hard work would be a powerful pacifier for workers confined to the least attractive jobs (Briggs, 1961, pp. 247–249; Rimlinger, 1971, p. 121). This elite necessity for stable economic incentives combines with the also universal mass demand for family security and social justice to make it necessary that the shock of mobility failures be cushioned and the risks of modern life be tempered. So pro-welfare-state doctrines are perhaps as widely popular as the ideology of success.

Collectivist sentiment and economic individualism can be tapped in the same interview at the same moment. For instance, Free and Cantril (1967, pp. 189–192) note a paradox in 1965 answers from "two regular Gallup samples . . . representing national cross-sections of the adult population. . . . Certain key questions were asked in both of the surveys, so that the total number of Americans interviewed reached 3,175." These polls clearly show wide acceptance of proposals for national health insurance, federal government responsibility to do away with poverty, and increased spending on urban renewal, along with majority sentiment that relief rolls are loaded with chiselers, that any able-bodied person who really wants to work can earn a living, and that we should rely more on individual initiative and less on welfare.

Results from American public-opinion polls suggest this underlying theme. Within the context of a diffuse success ideology, the adult population discriminates among welfare-state policies: if the beneficiaries seem to work for it (earnings-based pensions, prepaid medical insurance), it is good, and big majorities of the respondents in national cross-section samples generally support an actual or proposed program. If the benefit is unearned or perceived as unearned (AFDC, unemployment compensation), it is bad, and majorities typically reject the program.

37

That a benefit is, in fact, earned does not affect mass attitudes as much as the perceptions of how "needy" and "deserving" the beneficiaries are. Thus, popular support for old-age programs in the United States has been strong and appears to have increased since the Social Security Act of 1935, while support for unemployment compensation—which is, in fact, tied to worker earnings and paid by employers as part of current labor costs—is weak and appears to have gradually decreased since 1935 (Schiltz, 1970, p. 93). A poll conducted by Opinion Research Corporation in 1945 showed that about seven in ten of a national cross section of adults favored spending more money on "help for older people," compared with only three in ten who favored more money for "unemployment benefits" (Schiltz, 1970, p. 128). The reasons repeatedly appear in surveys over the past three decades: the suspicion that the unemployed are making joblessness a way of life or could really find work if they tried, while not as deep as the hostility to those on "public assistance" (like "welfare mothers"), is nevertheless widespread. For instance, in a 1965 national survey Gallup found that three-quarters of the respondents thought "many workers collect unemployment benefits when they could find work"—a suspicion shared by at least 60 percent of every category by age, education, income, occupation, and party affiliation (Schiltz, 1970, p. 160). A more intensive 1962 survey of public opinion in Ohio, a more modern, industrial state, uncovered a somewhat less harsh view: 38 percent of this cross section of adults endorsed the idea that unemployment is the "worker's own fault" while 45 percent allowed that unemployment is "usually beyond the worker's control" (Miller et al., 1963, p. 20). This rather even split between self-blame ("individualism") and system blame ("collectivism") also appears in surveys tapping reasons for individual poverty, with "lack of effort" mentioned about as often as "circumstances beyond their control" (Schiltz, 1970, p. 160).

To know whether these ideological ambiguities appear in other rich countries would require comparable national surveys

of mass and elite beliefs regarding particular issues and programs, with comparable breakdowns of most and least modern
populations (cross-tabulations by age, education, income, occupation, urban-rural experience)—studies not yet begun.

In sum, it is a mistake to peg "individualistic" values and beliefs as American or capitalist, and "collectivist" as European or socialist. Despite their apparent differences in welfare backlash, rich countries perhaps converge not only in types and coverage of welfare programs but also in the ideological reinforcements of those programs.

IDEOLOGY AND PRACTICE

Countries vary in the size of the universal gap between ideology and practice. Sweden and the USSR may represent extremes in the meshing of words and deeds: Sweden is most egalitarian in practice, and its political rhetoric comes close to its practice; the USSR is most egalitarian in ideology, and it is one of the least egalitarian in practice. The United States is far from the Soviet Union in its ideology, but closer in its practice. The failure to separate official rhetoric and popular sentiment from welfare practice creates great confusion in discussion of the welfare state.

For instance, Rimlinger argues that the insurance principle of relating benefits to earnings is individualistic, while the absence of a contractual element and reliance on the state is collectivistic, the keynote of Soviet welfare. He states that the absence of any contractual ties gives Soviet planners great leeway to control the income of all citizens to meet the needs of the state, the Communist Party, or the economy as they see them (1971, p. 253). But it turns out that they see such needs much as their Western counterparts do. In percentage of GNP spent on social security, the Soviet Union is closer to the United States than it is to Austria, the Netherlands, Sweden, or West Germany (see table 2). In the development of their welfare state, Soviet leaders gradually tightened service requirements in the granting of benefits, excluded the self-employed, and until 1964, excluded the mass of agricultural workers. Moreover, they adopted a general policy of linking benefits to earnings. All these policies, of course, make the Soviet Union resemble the United States.

Germany, which under Bismarck pioneered the welfare state, evidences a similar trend, with "laissez-faire" elements such as differentiated benefits and contributions side by side with a strong strain of collectivism and paternalism (Rimlinger, 1971, pp. 91, 98). Britain, although it is said to share the Anglo-American-French tradition of "individualism" and "liberalism" (pp. 336, 89), is also supposed to epitomize the egalitarian welfare state. Rimlinger observes that it has a tradition of flat benefits and flat contributions, accenting equal social rights regardless of earnings (p. 150). Yet we learn that, after World War II, Britain abandoned its egalitarianism and moved to wage-related pensions. Whatever its cultural traditions, by 1966 it ranked only tenth in social security spending among twenty-two rich countries (table 2). And by 1970 the home of Beveridge's uniform flat-rate benefit had extended earnings-related supplements from old-age pensions to unemployment and sickness benefits (Fisher, 1971, p. 23). Even Sweden, it appears, "which traditionally had adhered to a basic egalitarian benefit, has adopted differentiated benefits related to previous earnings" (Rimlinger, 1971, p. 342). There is now an organization of degree holders in Sweden, SACO, waging an aggressive campaign against the egalitarian notions of unions and their socialist allies. And after more than forty years of Social Democratic rule, the socialists were almost thrown out in the 1973 election.

The safest generalization about welfare ideology and practice is this: although doctrines vary and the welfare rhetoric of Prime Minister Edward Heath or President Nixon has been tougher than that of Olof Palme or Willy Brandt, the practice in every rich country fits a mixed mold. Gordon (1967, pp. 322–325) notes a decided tendency for industrial countries to

move toward dual systems of income maintenance for the aged,
and in some cases, also, for the survivors and the disabled. One
provides a minimum pension, which is egalitarian; the other, an
earnings-related pension, which supplements the minimum and
which is inegalitarian. If, like Great Britain, you start with a
contributory pension providing flat benefits, you later add either
a contributory earnings-related supplement or an income-conditioned pension or both. If, like Switzerland, you start with a
pension providing an earnings-related benefit, you later construct a better floor under it by adding an income-conditioned
minimum pension guarantee, similar to the systems of France,
Italy, and Czechoslovakia.

When ideology and practice are far apart, the chief
mechanism for reconciling them and getting on with the
business of solving real problems is back-door entry. The
principle of back-door entry is evident in Medicare and veterans'
programs in the United States and in family allowances everywhere.

Family allowances constitute a back door that opened wide.
In France, for example, family allowances were not established
as a direct move toward universal income maintenance; instead,
they were sold on pronatalist grounds (although there is no
evidence that child allowances increase fertility rates) and as
protection of the sacred—the nation and the family. A candid
effort to guarantee income to practically every adult whatever
his status or work contribution goes against the grain of
individualism; family allowances can serve a similar function
under the cover of an acceptable doctrine. Indeed, in several
rich countries in the early 1970s the revitalization of family
allowances as a back-door means of reducing poverty was the
focus of one of the livelier debates about the future of social
security (Fisher, 1971, p. 32).

Or consider veterans' pensions and welfare benefits in the
United States—a back door that never opened to anyone but
veterans. Compared with ordinary public relief or old-age
assistance, veterans' benefits pay better and come easier; the

recipients are not badgered or made to feel they are a drag on society. These programs are, in fact, the very model of a modern humanistic socialism: they are characterized by federal standards and financing; a presumption of eligibility and of earned right; easy application and easy appeals; and a warmhearted collaboration of intercessor groups like the American Legion, who drum up claimants, and an administrative agency instructed by law to follow its natural sympathies in favor of claims (Steiner, 1971, pp. 239–242). The symbol of the fighting man who was handicapped by his frontline injuries is steadily invoked to justify a straight welfare program to cover all veterans—battle-front or homefront, disabled or not, those with service-con-nected disabilities, those whose deprivations developed long after or before brief periods of service, as well as those who suffered no deprivations at all.

Finally, consider Medicare, the back door that stands ajar. After decades of futile struggle to pass a national health-insur-ance program in the United States, this limited program for the aged was piggybacked onto the more popular system of Old-Age Survivors and Disability Insurance. Senator Edward Kennedy's national health-insurance proposals are similarly tied to the OASDI system in order to conform to the tough-minded myth that no one will get something for nothing. Especially where the ideology of economic individualism is strong must the practice enter the back door, dressed up to fit existing values and beliefs.

IDEOLOGY VERSUS ECONOMIC LEVEL AND POLITICAL SYSTEM: AN EMPIRICAL TEST

To determine the effect of ideology on the development of the welfare state, we devised a complex measure of the ideological stance of the ruling parties or dominant coalitions in twenty-two countries from 1950 through 1965 on five issues centered around equality.[9] Four comprise an index of belief in planning for

9. Data on ideology came from Kenneth Janda (1970), the International Comparative Political Parties Project, a large-scale comparative study of eleven

equality; one is an indicator of belief in equality of opportunity. Janda (1970) reports a factor analysis of thirteen issue scores for twenty-six political parties for twelve countries. Six issues tapped an underlying dimension which he calls "left-right." This factor is comprised of party positions on redistribution of wealth, government ownership, central economic planning, and social welfare plus secularization of society, and East-West alignment. Two other issue orientations have weak negative loadings with this left-right factor: equality of opportunity ($-.17$) and support of the military ($-.35$). Janda gives each party a score ranging from $+5$ (pro) to -5 (anti). The party scores in the twenty-two countries analyzed here tend to cluster toward the left or positive, so the zero point is more "conservative" than "moderate."

Since we were interested in measuring the ideological stance of governing elites regarding the welfare state, equality, and war, we used the following items (only the positive extreme is reported here in Janda's phrasing):

1. *Providing for Social Welfare.* Advocates or supports universally available social welfare through a compulsory program of public assistance, including aid to the poor, unemployed, aged, and health care and medical benefits.
2. *Redistribution of Wealth.* Advocates severe redistribution from rich

---

dimensions of parties, one of which is issue orientation. I am grateful for his generosity in supplying computer printout of his scores for each of 154 political parties in fifty-two countries as well as codes for each issue with coding confidence ratings. The product-moment reliability coefficient between two sets of "blind" coders for all his issue orientations averaged .86. We were able to use data for twenty-two of these countries. Twelve are rich countries of table 2: Australia, Austria, Denmark, East Germany, West Germany, Ireland, the Netherlands, New Zealand, Sweden, the USSR, the United Kingdom, and the United States. The others are Bulgaria, Greece (pre-junta), India, Luxembourg, Nicaragua, Paraguay, Portugal, Tunisia, Turkey, and Uruguay. Janda's sample of fifty-two eliminates countries that had no functioning parties of any sort during 1950–1962 (e.g., Libya, Ethiopia, Haiti). The sample bias for our sub-set is against (1) countries in which military coups or large-scale revolutions have occurred or (2) countries that achieved independence after 1950. In any case, these excluded countries are typically very poor, or spend very little on social security, or both.

to poor; suggestions for major land reform and equalization of all incomes; demands that redistributions be immediate; combined seizure and redistribution.

3. *Economic Planning.* Advocates government prescription of the level and nature of resource allocation, commodity production, and distribution. Often represented by the promulgation of "five-year plans" and the like.

4. *Government Ownership of Means of Production.* Strongly favors government ownership: advocates government ownership of all basic industries; advocates government ownership of means of production generally.

5. *Allocation of Resources to Armed Forces.* Promilitary: favors greater infusion of resources into armed forces or increase in expenditures to achieve pervasive security against perceived foreign or domestic enemies; military budget given priorities over domestic programs, with little questioning of underlying assumptions.

6. *Equality of Opportunity* (Janda calls this "protection of civil rights"). Advocates a government policy of outlawing discrimination broadly across social life and providing for enforcement of the policy.

We computed a composite score for each country on each of these six issues, using a weighted average of the ruling parties or coalitions for every year from 1950 through 1965 as follows: (1) note the ruling party or coalition for each year (source: Mallory, 1950–1965); (2) record the Janda score for the ruling party for each year for each issue; (3) where there are ruling coalitions—typical of European parliamentary governments—compute a weighted average of the Janda scores for the parties that form the coalition (the weight for each party is the number of the seats it holds as a fraction of the number of seats the ruling coalition holds); (4) add the issue scores for each year and divide the total ruling party or coalition score by the total number of years (sixteen).[10]

10. Because of missing data on Janda scores, the final table has eighteen empty cells (14 percent of the data units). In constructing the index of planning for equality, which is coherent, missing cells were assigned the average score for that country for the other issues. If data were missing for the indicator of equality of opportunity, we eliminated the country.

For the purpose of the present analysis these averages are interpreted as a measure of the dominant or composite ideological stance of a country during the period of welfare-state development covered in table 2. The data base for Janda's scores was more than 60,000 pages of verbal output—mostly monographic accounts of party positions but also official rhetoric in party platforms, campaign literature, press releases, speeches, newspaper reports. Although Janda does adjust a party's ideological score in favor of party practice where discrepancies between the two are apparent, his definition of action is vague and depends largely on verbal statements. It is our impression that the effect of practice on ideology in the actual coding is not great. In any case, to the extent that party action does contaminate these measures of ideology, readers who think that values are best revealed in action cannot argue that the Janda scores stack the case against the power of ideology.

To assure the coherence and independence of our measures, we did a factor analysis on these country scores for six issues, using a varimax rotation. It confirmed Janda's results for party scores: the four planning-for-equality items strongly hang together (loadings range from .85 to .89); scores for equality of opportunity and support for the military form an orthogonal factor, strong support for equal opportunity (+.89) going together with strong antimilitary views (−.87).

I took these pains to measure elite ideology so that I could provide a fair test of my prediction that, for the reasons discussed above, ideology would not explain national differences in social security spending. Regression analyses demonstrate clearly and consistently that ideology has no effect; the beta weights, like the zero-order correlations, are all insignificant when in the presence of economic level or its correlates, age of the social security system, and percentage of old people. The path diagrams in figures 2 and 3 report the results of two of these tests. For fourteen countries, equality of opportunity (whose zero-order correlations range from −.22 with planning for equality to +.24 for per capita GNP, neither significant) has no effect in a regression with planning for equality, per capita GNP, age of population, and age of system. For twenty-two countries, planning for equality (zero-order correlations range from −.15 with per capita GNP to +.22 with military spending, neither significant) has no effect in a regression with per capita GNP, military spending, age of population, and age of system.

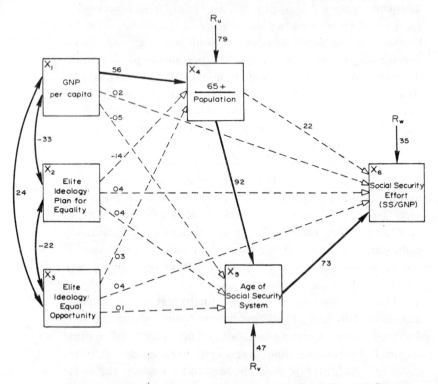

FIGURE 2. Causal Model of Social Security Spending: 14 Countries. Solid lines indicate relationships with p < .05; dotted lines indicate nonsignificant relationships.

In these path diagrams, insignificant path coefficients are designated by dotted lines. Once again, as in the earlier analysis of sixty countries, military effort is unrelated to social security effort. Again the line of influence runs from per capita income through proportion of aged in the population and age of system to social security effort. The model in figure 2 accounts for 88 percent of the variance in social security effort; the model in figure 3 accounts for 87 percent of the variance. The main story of these two path diagrams is the irrelevance of either measure of ideology and the consistent power of economic level and its demographic and bureaucratic correlates as predictors of welfare effort.

Summary and Interpretation. From previous comparative studies of both cross-sectional and time-series data and from my analysis of the social security spending of sixty countries in 1966, I am confident that figure 1 is a model that makes most theoretical sense and provides the best explanation of welfare effort for many countries with a wide spread of economic levels. The squared multiple correlation coefficient of 83 percent is impressive; there is not much variance left to explain. Results are consistent with or without inclusion of ideology, political system, or military spending.

Over the long pull, economic level is the root cause of welfare-state development, but its effects are felt chiefly through demographic changes of the past century and the momentum of the programs themselves, once established. With modernization, birth rates declined, and the proportion of aged was thereby increased. This increased importance of the aged, coupled with the declining economic value of children, in turn exerted pressure for welfare spending. Once the programs were established they matured, everywhere moving toward wider coverage and higher benefits. Social security growth begins as a natural accompaniment of economic growth and its demographic outcomes; it is hastened by the interplay of political elite perceptions, mass pressures, and welfare bureaucracies.

If there is one source of welfare spending that is most powerful—a single proximate cause—it is the proportion of old people in the population. The welfare state is a symbol of the ambiguous position of the aged in modern society, both dependent and independent, a minority of strategic importance in public spending.

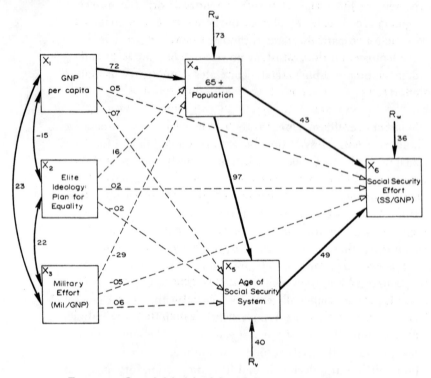

FIGURE 3. Causal Model of Social Security Spending: 22 Countries. Solid lines indicate relationships with $p < .05$; dotted lines indicate nonsignificant relationships.

Insofar as political system apart from economic level shapes this process, the two dominant modern systems, totalitarianism and liberal democracy, work in the same direction—boosting spending a bit—via their influence on demographic structure. Totalitarian governments, more centralized, have an edge in this generally limited positive influence.

Our two measures of ideology (the index of belief in "planning for equality" and the belief in "equality of opportunity") consistently add nothing. In this cross-sectional analysis, level of military spending also adds nothing, although under some conditions, discussed in chapter 4, it can subvert welfare spending. On the basis of Pryor's comparison of seven market economies and seven centralized economies (1968), we can conclude that economic system, too, is irrelevant.

In response to similar problems of providing economic and career incentives and maintaining political order under conditions of the general push for equality and social justice and specific concern about the aged, all rich countries develop a similar set of conflicting values and beliefs—welfare-state ideologies versus "free mobility" or "success" ideologies. For the same reasons, there is a general convergence of social security practice toward dual systems of income maintenance. To understand the major differences in welfare-state effort, administration, and output, therefore, we must look not to these broad, self-canceling, ideological themes but to more concrete, sharper contrasts in social, political, and economic organization. For at the level of affluence achieved by the twenty-two richest countries in the world, we find both convergence and divergence, unexplained by a model covering the time span of a century and embracing Sweden and Tunisia, Denmark and Bulgaria, the USSR and India.

3

Diversity and Uniformity among Rich Countries

Leaving aside education, and controlling for the age of the system and the age of the population, what structural attributes of rich countries other than economic level can explain the impressive variations in welfare spending among the twenty-two countries in table 2?

My guiding hypotheses are that variations in both welfare-state practice and ideology can be explained by variations in (1) political centralization as it relates to (2) social heterogeneity and internal cleavages, (3) stratification and mobility (especially the position of middle strata), (4) the size of the working class and the nature of its organization, and (5) the influence of the military. I suggest that if rich countries become more alike in these attributes of structure, they will develop similar welfare-state practices and ideologies. If they become less alike in structure, their unique histories and cultures will have greater force and their welfare systems will become more diverse.

Ideology in this scheme is both a dependent variable, which is explained by such attributes of structure, and a weaker independent variable, which at once causes and reflects the amount and type of welfare spending. A people accustomed to big spending who also like its results will develop a pro-welfare-state ideology and will more readily pay for further expansion of services, including income-equalizing benefits.

This chapter presents concepts and measures of social structure which I believe useful for cross-national studies not only of the welfare state but of other patterns of behavior, too. Having shown the severe limits of global concepts of ideology, political system, and economic system so popular among both social scientists and their wider audiences, I now aim to present alternative ideas of social structure that permit a more disciplined, systematic comparison of nations. More specifically, I shall present interrelated hypotheses that fit the data in tables 2, 3, and 4, and that can be supported or contradicted, at least illustratively, by comparative studies of two or more rich countries. Together, these hypotheses constitute what Robert Merton calls a "theory of the middle range"—by far the most powerful kind of theory sociologists have thus far produced. Theories of bureaucracy, of deviance, of popular culture, of the welfare state, to me, need not explain everything in the social universe. It is enough if such theories present propositions that are sufficiently interrelated to be coherent, sufficiently concrete to be tested, and sufficiently "relevant" to explain a recurrent phenomenon about which both scholars and other citizens can remain excited for more than a passing generation. This chapter, then, aims to locate specific attributes of structure that can explain variations in welfare-state development among the twenty-two richest countries in the world.[1]

STRUCTURAL EXPLANATIONS IN THE MIDDLE RANGE

It is predicted that, among rich countries, the conditions outlined below will lead both to the most developed welfare

1. The further systematic test of these hypotheses in the style of chapter 2 is in progress; over the next several years the results will be combined with intensive case studies of the political economy of welfare spending and administration among selected welfare-state leaders and laggards. To facilitate discussion of their interrelations, I shall number the five groups of hypotheses below. Within each group, the notation indicates hypotheses of increasing concreteness and specificity.

state (i.e., one with high levels of spending on welfare, health, and related services, program emphasis on income-equalizing benefits, generous rather than punitive administration) and to the most powerful supporting ideologies.

1. Centralization, social heterogeneity, and internal cleavages.

1.1. *Degree of centralization of government, whatever the political system. Hypothesis: The greater the authority of the central government vis-à-vis regional and local units, the higher the welfare-state spending and the greater the program emphasis on equality.* Political elites who embrace the welfare state in centralized polities can better overcome resistance to the necessary taxes and expenditures than elites in decentralized polities. Preliminary analysis supports this hypothesis. We devised an index of centralization that weighs the economic clout of the central government (central government revenues as a share of total government revenues) four times as heavily as formal structure (unitary versus federal; and central government appointment of chief executives of provinces, districts, and counties versus selection by council or popular election).

Of the top nine welfare-state leaders in table 2, six are clearly among the nine most centralized governments (Belgium, the Netherlands, France, Italy, East Germany, and Czechoslovakia) and one is ambiguous (Sweden, with a medium score on centralization). Of the seven countries ranked lowest in social security, four are among the least centralized (Switzerland, Canada, the United States, Australia) and one is ambiguous (Japan, with a medium score on centralization). For this one hypothesis, Israel and the USSR spend too little for their high degree of centralization: West Germany and Austria spend too much for their low scores on centralization.

A major explanation for the deviance of Israel and the USSR is their heavy military burden, which at that extreme plainly retards welfare-state development (see hypothesis 5 in chapter 4, and the trend data in tables 2 and 3). The negligible military burden of Austria and the moderate one of West

Germany, however, cannot explain their large social security effort because they each have counterparts at the same level of military spending who spend much less on social security. That they were pioneers in social security history (they score high on the index of age of system) and fit the rest of my hypotheses well can better explain these two cases, which in some measure contradict the idea that centralization fosters welfare spending.

1.2. *Social heterogeneity and internal cleavages.* This is Myrdal's explanation of the backwardness of the United States (1960, pp. 54ff., 87, 100 passim). *Hypothesis* (see Wilensky, 1965, pp. xvii–xviii): *No pattern will be evident because of the contradictory pressures of minority groups.*

On the one hand, a wider civic virtue cannot fully flourish when ties to minority groups are strong, for racial, ethnic-linguistic, and religious cleavages block meaningful participation in less parochial voluntary associations and encourage separatist allegiances; further, minority groups sometimes create welfare and education services of their own, thereby subverting public expenditures (see hypothesis 2.1.7). On the other hand, minority groups create general pressure for equality and sometimes seek expanded state aid for education and welfare services.

If these contradictory pressures offset one another, there will be no pattern. Again, without intensive investigation, we apparently have homogeneous, high-spending Sweden, Italy, and Germany versus heterogeneous, low-spending United States, Switzerland, Canada, and maybe the USSR. But offsetting this pattern is the high spending of heterogeneous Belgium and the Netherlands, where structural cleavages enhance support for the welfare state, the medium rank of homogeneous Denmark, Norway, Finland, and the United Kingdom, and the low spending of homogeneous Japan.

1.2.1. *Social heterogeneity and internal cleavages slow down welfare-state development only where they are given sharp expression by a decentralized, if not fragmented, polity.* (Hypothesis 2.1 and Wilensky, 1965, p. xix.) Consider two countries at the extremes of spending, both with very strong religious cleavages—the Netherlands at the top, the United States at the bottom. In the Netherlands one needs a special vocabulary (*verzuiling* or "pillarization," "view of life," "confessional-political blocs") to describe the diversity of religious and nonreligious groups which cut through all areas of Dutch life and are expressed in social issues. Even radio and television are organized by these blocs. A strong central government, however, is able to channel their expression and dampen the cleavages. The provinces and municipalities are weak; their heads are appointed at The Hague; government integrates the confessional-political blocs at the top in a complex network of advisory bodies, public and semipublic (Goudsblom, 1967). The welfare state flourishes. A similar central containment of more bitter ethnic-linguistic struggles is evident in Belgium. The contrast of Holland and Belgium with the decentralized and fragmented federalism of the United States, Switzerland, or Canada is obvious.

The above hypotheses refer only to that social heterogeneity based on descent (ethnicity, religion, race). Other sources of heterogeneity—education, occupation, income—are covered in hypotheses 2 and 3 below.

2. Stratification and mobility.

2.1. *Levels of affluence and opportunities of the reluctant majority, especially the size, economic position, and relative tax burden of the "middle mass"* (upper working class and lower middle class).[2] *Hypotheses: Correlates of affluence—a growing middle mass, greater educational and occupational opportunity—will foster anti-welfare-state ideologies. The anti-welfare effects of affluence will be strengthened whenever the middle mass perceives the financing or distribution of services as inequitable.* Specifically,

2.1.1. *The greater the educational opportunity* (measured

2. For discussion of the concept of the middle mass, see Wilensky, 1960, pp. 552, 558; 1961, pp. 524, 529–530, 539; and chapter 5 below.

by enrollment rates or fraction of the children of lower strata who go on to higher education), the more chance that the middle-mass parents of college students as well as a large number of the highly educated will resist the push from below for equality.

Consistent with this hypothesis are scattered data on the fraction of students in higher education from "working-class families" (very likely upper-working-class plus some white-collar workers), reported by OECD (Conference, 1971, table B, p. 56). Of seven welfare-state leaders for which data are available for the mid-sixties, four provide extremely limited educational opportunity for workers' children (Germany, Austria, France, the Netherlands, ranging from 5.3 to 9.4 percent) and two offer middling opportunity (Sweden 14.3, Italy 15.4). Only Belgium seems to score high both on welfare spending and on the percentage of students of working-class origin (22.8), but both that figure and Italy's are inflated because they are confined to the percentage of new entrants. (Cf. Poignant, 1965, 194–202, 270–273.) The data, however, are merely suggestive.

2.1.2. The *higher the rate of occupational mobility*, the more chance that the mobile population will adhere to the success ideology (the values and beliefs of economic individualism discussed above). Illustrative evidence consistent with this hypothesis comes from a table which compares intergenerational occupational mobility from manual to nonmanual strata for four of our twenty-two countries (Fox and Miller, 1965, p. 2). The rates are high for the United States, quite high for Great Britain and Japan (which rank low to medium in welfare spending) and low for the Netherlands (which ranks high in welfare spending).

2.1.2.1. Holding economic level constant, *the more rapid the rate of economic growth*, the greater the educational and occupational opportunities for the middle mass, and thus the greater their resistance to paying for those who fall behind. Swift increase in per capita income, in a situation of obviously expanding opportunity, slows down welfare-state development.

55

On the other hand, the more opportunity, the more chance that a committed political elite will be able to raise taxes for the welfare state, which should, on average, attenuate the relationship between rapid rates of economic growth and slow rates of welfare-state development.

There may be a U-curve of growth and related resistance, however. With high growth rates the affluent mobile majority are not eager to redistribute downward. At the other extreme of *no* growth—the situation of Europe and Japan as the energy crisis ·went public in 1974—a similar hardening of resistance is evident; for then, whatever the poor gain from welfare expenditures, the non-poor lose, and a Hobbesian state of mind spreads.

2.1.2.2. *The income distribution and tax system at the beginning of a period of rapid growth* will condition the relationship between growth and the tax take, and hence government capacity to spend. For instance, much of the lower strata may be so poor and tax exemptions so generous that growth causes only a small population to achieve enough income to attract tax attention. Put another way, the effect of rapid rates of growth on welfare spending depends in part on the *revenue elasticity of taxes*—their sensitivity to growth.

2.1.2.3. *Very high levels of growth increase the revenue elasticity of taxes; rapid rates of growth together with high revenue elasticity greatly increases the capacity of committed elites to collect and spend for welfare purposes.* Therefore, hypothesis 2.1.2.1—growth increases mass resistance—will hold best for the early period of social security development and for the moderately affluent countries when taxes are harder to collect. At some advanced level, the economy becomes so complex and rationalized, large-scale organizations so dominant, and record-keeping so extensive, that it is easier to collect head taxes—for instance, employer and worker contributions. At that level, rapid rates of growth enhance social security spending. (This is consistent with the results on level of growth in table 1—the big jump in social security spending from the third quartile of per capita income to the second—but inconsistent with the hypothesis of a slowdown in the rate of increase of welfare spending among the richest countries, which depends on the force of other variables.)

Because data on rates of economic growth are better than data on occupational mobility, and because swift growth is known to enhance occupational opportunity, we may be forced to rely on growth rates as a substitute for social mobility, directly measuring social mobility in only the few countries where the data are passably comparable.

2.1.3. *The greater the visible tax burden of the middle mass relative to the upper middle class and the rich, the greater the resistance to health and welfare spending that appears to favor the poor.* While middle-mass response to tax inequities may include some anger toward upper-strata "fat cats," the basic identification of the middle mass is upward and across, not down, so their resentment is projected onto lower strata. I emphasize perceived inequities, but I assume that these are related in moderate measure to the actual tax structure and distribution of benefits.

2.1.4. *The more social distance between the middle mass and the poor, the greater the resistance to spending that appears to favor the poor.* Blacks in the United States, "guest workers" in Switzerland, and Francophones in Canada provide ready examples of populations that have been seen as both strange and poor and treated accordingly. As Spaniards, Italians, and Yugoslavs push up into the building trades and tourist trades in Switzerland, they provoke the same anxious reaction among the established middle mass as the blacks pressing for equality in the United States. For instance, a 1970 national referendum in Switzerland which proposed to limit the admission of foreign workers got the support of 46 percent of the total vote. (See also hypothesis 1.2.1.)

Like the Man Who Came to Dinner and stayed for several months, the guest workers of Europe are increasingly settling down in the host countries for long periods, even their whole working lives (Castles and Kosack, 1973, pp. 54–56). The

interests of such long-term migrants are to get out of the
unattractive jobs in which they are concentrated—semiskilled
work on assembly lines, street cleaning, garbage collection, other
municipal services—and to move up to higher-paid supervisory
and skilled jobs (Ball, 1973). Workers in the host country, of
course, resist such incursions into their territory.

This competition between natives and strangers has also
emerged in the United Kingdom, where both foreign workers
from mainland Europe and Commonwealth immigrants (mostly
Asians and black West Indians) have come to England. The
political popularity of Enoch Powell, the classically educated
George Wallace of the Midlands, reflects British workers'
growing resentment toward the newcomers. Resentment toward
nonwhite immigrants was recently given expression in legislation
tightening restrictions on entry.

When the bloom of growth is off (2.1.2.1), these normal
majority-minority tensions increase and the agitation to send the
guests home intensifies. Since World War II, the major
European users of the 7.5 million officially counted foreign
workers—West Germany, East Germany, France, Great Britain,
Switzerland, Austria, Sweden, Belgium, the Netherlands, Luxembourg—have been in a position to shift their poverty problem
to their guests and, they thought, to export their unemployment
problems in bad times. But both the countries supplying foreign
labor and the guest workers themselves have pressed for equity
in housing, schools, and welfare benefits—which implies the
special attention and funding needed by culturally handicapped
minority groups everywhere. And the economic slumps, instead
of inspiring the guest workers with an acquiescent willingness to
go home, made most of them hold still more tenaciously to their
jobs. For instance, during the German recession of 1966–67,
while 300,000 foreigners went home, a million stayed to work,
some of them more secure in their jobs than German workers.
The multiple economic crises of the mid-seventies are inten-
sifying middle-mass resistance to both the presence and the
equitable treatment of guest workers.

2.1.5. *Systems of contributory financing and indirect taxation are less visible and evoke less political resistance to health and welfare spending than systems which rely heavily on direct taxes.* There is evidence of a general "collectivization" of life in twenty-two noncommunist countries; from 1955 to 1969 "pure" private consumption expenditures—what is left after taxes, savings, and government transfers—as a fraction of GNP declined 6.6 percent (OECD, 1972, p. 50). And everywhere social security spending increases faster than GNP, while inflation accelerates. People are happy to consume government services but increasingly restive about paying for them.

In these circumstances, political elites in rich countries have only a few broad fiscal alternatives: increase direct taxes such as taxes on income and property; increase indirect taxes such as sales taxes and the value-added tax; increase social security contributions of employers or employees or both; reduce tax cheating; radically increase the efficiency of programs and services; cut benefits directly or hold them below the level of inflation, thereby cutting them indirectly.

There may be an interdependence of several of these strategies which fosters big welfare spending: increased reliance on indirect taxes which are less visible; increased employer contributions, which workers view as great victories but which can readily be passed on in increased prices; or increased worker contributions, which, although they should be visible, are typically given general labels and are mysteriously forgotten in the intense focus on take-home pay; and tolerance of a high rate of tax evasion, which provides psychological comfort to those who simultaneously feel most squeezed and cheat with greatest ingenuity. (Thus, farmers, artisans, and small entrepreneurs in service industries, rather than mounting the barricades, will feel, with some justification, that they are beating the system.) Finally, instead of cutting benefits, this strategy redistributes resources among competing programs by letting inflation erode programs with the least political force. Conversely, few governments move boldly to increase direct taxes, crack down on tax evaders and cheaters, and directly cut benefits.

The countries with the greatest tax-evasion rates, according to European budget officials and government economists whom I interviewed, are Italy, France, Belgium, and Austria—all among the top spenders. They are also those with the greatest reliance on either indirect taxes or contributory systems of financing (France leads in both). These tendencies are consistent with my location of greatest tax resistance in the middle mass. Even small increments of direct taxes can hurt these people, who see the money deducted from their paychecks; large segments of the lower class pay little or are exempt; while large segments of the upper middle class and the rich can, with the help of tax advisers, avoid payment.

In this picture of popular response to contributory taxes, the greatest puzzle is why so many hardworking citizens of the middle mass accept with equanimity heavy payroll deductions labeled "social insurance" and yet at the same time rebel against similar, even smaller, income-tax deductions. Both taxes, it would appear, are equally visible, cut right out of the paycheck. Recent developments in the United States provide an example of mass obliviousness to the real impact of taxes. At the end of 1973, millions of workers were paying nothing at all under the progressive income-tax schedule, but these same workers saw 5.85 percent of their income deducted from their paychecks in a regressive flat rate for social security (cf. Pechman, 1971, p. 174, figure 7.2), which provoked no great restiveness. In November 1973, the United States Senate actually passed an amendment to a social security bill which would have refunded from general revenues the entire social security tax for most workers earning up to an annual wage of $4,000. The poorer the worker, the larger his refund; past an income of $5,600, no refund check would be received. At this writing, the bill is still to be considered by the House of Representatives, but the usual furor about unearned rights is assured. The social security expert of the AFL-CIO, who might be expected to support such a reduction in regressivity, opposed the bill because it would begin to "break the link between social-security taxes and an *earned* right to benefits" (*New York Times*, December 9, 1973). This illusion that social security taxes, however regressive, are paid for benefits duly and directly received, while an income tax is lost to the winds, is a crucial reinforcement for regressive features of welfare-state financing.

To gauge resistance to various combinations of taxes and benefits and thereby grasp the potential for education in distributive justice, we need intensive examination of mass and elite beliefs and values concerning various systems of financing and taxation, visible and invisible.

2.1.6. *The larger the percent of the labor force who have had a taste of self-employment, the greater the economic individualism and concomitant resistance to the welfare state.* Reinforcing the ideology and marginal position of *les indé-pendants* (or *les classes moyennes*) are administrative difficulties in extending social security to them; governments everywhere have trouble collecting either employer contributions or social security taxes from many scattered small shops and stores.

Independent proprietors, rural or nonrural, epitomize those occupational opportunities (hypothesis 2.1.2) and sentiments about the tax squeeze (2.1.3) that foster economic individualism. Solo professionals too—at least where they are numerous and well organized as in the United States and Canada—share the ideology of the artisans and entrepreneurs of the middle mass.

Expressions of the hostility of the self-employed to the state in general and the welfare state in particular abound: the Poujadiste movement in France and its successors, such as the Conféderation générale des petites et moyennes Enterprises, the Union de Défense des Commerçants et Artisans, the Union nationale des Travailleurs indépendants, and the Comité d'In-formation et de Défense; some elements of the neo-Fascist vote in Italy (e.g., shopkeepers and solo professionals in small towns); parts of Governor Ronald Reagan's constituency in California (e.g., land speculators, realtors, used-car dealers); landowning

61

wage-workers in Switzerland; and the numerous managers and owners of tiny industrial workshops in Japan, who have recently organized a "small and medium scale industrial union" to resist government interference.

The ideology and political direction of the self-employed vary from country to country, but there are several roads to resistance. Austria, for instance, is at first glance a negative case for my hypothesis. Self-employed professionals such as doctors and lawyers are weak; they are regulated by a powerful public bureaucracy. The numerous shopkeepers, organized around a corporate Catholic ideology, have achieved protective legislation, favorable taxation, and local control of entry. Still, these shopkeepers, a power in the Austrian People's Party, are against too much welfare spending. Clinging to their traditional beliefs, they have not yet organized efficient welfare programs of their own (see hypothesis 2.1.7).

To demonstrate the political role of the self-employed as a source of resistance to welfare spending, we must go beyond the simple rate of self-employment. It is true that in the long run, with continued economic growth, self-employed workers decline as a fraction of the civilian labor force. Unpaid family workers also decline. Further, some low or medium welfare spenders (the United States and the United Kingdom) have the smallest ratio of self-employed among the countries in table 2, while some big spenders (Italy, Belgium) have high rates of self-employment (Denison, 1967, p. 208). But these facts are misleading; they obscure the politically relevant work experience of the population.

For instance, the American economy has cast up a large minority who were brought up in entrepreneurial families or themselves have had (or will have) a taste of entrepreneurship before their working lives are over, or both. The fraction of the American urban labor force that have had businesses of their own for at least some of their working lives could not be less than a quarter. Even the rate of nonagricultural self-employment remained steady at about 10 percent from 1940 to 1963.

(For data on the size, persistence, importance, and discrete social character of self-employment, see Wilensky, 1966a, pp. 100–101, 112–114.)

Unfortunately, I have not discovered data linking self-employment experience to welfare-state attitudes for any country, let alone studies of the ideological effects of work histories in two or more countries with contrasting opportunities for self-employment. As a substitute measure of self-employment experience I tried to combine rates of current self-employment with bankruptcy rates for small businesses, but the concept of bankruptcy is too variable and the data are too weak.

The self-employment hypothesis may in any case be more persuasive in explaining national differences in the historical development of the welfare state than in its immediate future. For at some high level of welfare spending, *les indépendants* eventually join and demand their share. Poujadism at that level takes the form "We pay, you collect pensions, and we get nothing." In the early 1950s the self-employed of Belgium were a major source of diffuse and disorganized resistance to welfare spending; now they are well organized and are demanding that the government accept a greater share of the financing of social insurance. The strike of *les indépendants* in Belgium in October 1972 expressed their resistance to the red tape of the value-added tax and, more generally, to increased state control; also articulated, however, was a demand for participation in welfare and economic policy. Still hostile to labor unions and socialism, aware that they are a declining group, the Belgian self-employed are now more ambivalent, wondering what benefits they themselves can derive from the welfare state. Reflecting this new situation, coverage of social security is everywhere gradually spreading to the self-employed (Fisher, 1971, p. 7).

2.1.7. *The extent to which private welfare benefits have been elaborated along with the public benefits. Hypothesis: in terms of public opinion, lush private benefits foster the cheerful illusion that stingy public programs are adequate* (Wilensky, 1965, p. xvi); *in terms of economics, the substitution effects*

63

*between public and private health and welfare expenditures are
very large.*

In every rich country of the West, proliferation of private
welfare measures that tend to increase inequality accompanies
the expansion of public welfare measures that function to
reduce inequality. Consider the vast array of "occupational
welfare benefits" employers have adopted: pensions, death
benefits, cash sickness benefits, sick leave, medical care, travel
expenses, meals, cars, houses, credit cards, cheap loans, school
fees, season tickets, holiday expenses and vacation resorts,
education and training grants. Most of these benefits are types
of untaxed or lightly taxed "income"; their ultimate cost is thus
borne by the government (Titmuss, 1958, p. 69). Most important for the issue of equality, these fringe benefits are typically
tied to employment, seniority, and occupational achievement;
employees already well-off receive a disproportionate share of
both hard cash and subtle amenities. The privileged access of a
Soviet manager or Party official to a dacha or a Black Sea resort
is perhaps the Communist equivalent, which, if developed on a
grand scale, may have similar effects.

Although comparative data on private benefit plans are
weak, it is likely that (1) there is a tendency common to modern
societies for an increasing proportion of total wages and salaries
to be paid in the form of fringe benefits; and, less surely, (2) the
greater the employer contributions to nonstatutory social security schemes, the less the fraction of national income devoted to
public welfare programs. It appears that the United States has
traveled furthest down this anti-egalitarian path: our contributions to employee benefit plans in relation to national income
are larger than those in other rich countries, but our expenditure
on social security and private plans combined is nevertheless
lower (Gordon, 1963, pp. 21–23).

Private insurance, bought out-of-pocket by individuals,
apparently has the same dampening effect. Pryor reports such an
effect in the United States, especially the subversion of public
health expenditures by private health insurance, although there

is some evidence of similar substitution effects across many countries for health, welfare, and education alike (1968, pp. 143–144, 292).

Private schemes may be growing among both welfare-state leaders and laggards. It is extremely difficult to sort out their effects. Private schemes have become part of the compulsory public system in France. Private medical plans and life insurance are spreading in Austria; they supplement public benefits and are tax exempt. The intensive studies required to assess the hypothesis of the mutual subversion of public and private under varying conditions of tax policy and private sponsorship have not been done. Development of the private welfare state may be a major source of resistance to further expansion of the public welfare state.

To recapitulate these stratification hypotheses: A large and growing middle mass (hypothesis 2.1) unaccustomed to big welfare spending, which enjoys many private benefits (2.1.7) and relatively good educational and occupational opportunities (2.2.1; 2.1.2), which is taxed visibly and directly (2.1.5) and feels its tax burden to be inequitable (2.1.3), which can displace its political frustration onto a socially distant poor (2.1.4), and which numbers in its ranks many entrepreneurs, past and present (2.1.6), will be a powerful brake on welfare-state development. The United States seems to fit. Perhaps Sweden's middle mass, despite its much heavier tax burden and similar opportunity structure, not only has been habituated to the welfare state but does not feel deprived relative to the even more heavily taxed upper strata.

3. The size of the working class and the nature of its organization.

Hypotheses: A large, strongly organized working class with high rates of participation in working-class organizations such as unions, churches, co-ops, leisure and other voluntary associations *fosters pro-welfare-state ideologies and big spending.*

3.1. *Whatever their form, the strength of working-class-based organizations is significant.* Whether the working class is

65

organized along socialist lines (strong socialist movements in the past and great electoral strength in the present, as in Italy, Sweden, and France) or along religious, linguistic, or other lines (as in the Netherlands and Belgium) is irrelevant. What counts is the strength of the collective push for equality.

3.2. *Participatory democracy in the administration of welfare schemes further enhances the influence of a strongly organized working class.* When the welfare state is highly developed—partly as a result of working-class pressure—it then provides additional channels for participation by working-class activists. Especially in Germany, France, Belgium, Sweden, and Austria have participatory administrative structures been created, adding impetus to the demand for expanded benefits, more generously given. Workers in such countries elect hundreds of representatives to administrative commissions running a variety of programs—in medical insurance, unemployment and accident insurance, and pensions. The unemployment insurance fund in Sweden, for instance, is strictly controlled and administered by labor unions in local communities, who jealously guard their autonomy.

If we contrast welfare-state laggards, we may find the obverse: a welfare state in which channels for participation are dominated by the upper middle class. In the United States, for instance, boards of control of local community social agencies have long been controlled by business executives and their wives plus physicians and attorneys (Wilensky and Lebeaux, 1958, pp. 269ff.), although that private welfare structure is in the process of opening up to other groups, especially racial minorities. Perhaps the traditional accent on the local autonomy of school districts in the United States is another expression of a welfare state structured for upper-middle-class participation.

In short, the welfare-state leaders invite union leaders and worker activists to help run the welfare show, the welfare-state laggards invite activists among professionals and managers to help run the education show—a possibility consistent with the finding that among rich countries social security effort is inversely related to enrollments in higher education (chapter 1).

Reliable, directly relevant comparative data on organizations with a working-class base or on participation rates of workers relative to the rest of the population do not exist. For work in process, we are relying on indirect measures which we think will capture the necessary variation for almost all of our twenty-two countries: "Left" voting, voter turnout, union membership ratios, and rough measures of the size of the working class. For a few countries, occasional comparative studies of particular communities or factories or aspects of working-class life and labor history will supplement these more quantitative data and provide negative and positive evidence bearing on the working class as a force in welfare-state development.

3.3. *The actual effect of the welfare state on income distribution is less important as a source of working-class support for it than the perception that it does something for them.*

Perhaps France best illustrates the necessity of distinguishing redistributional effects from egalitarian popular attitudes. A common phrase to describe government welfare policy is *saupoudrer*—to sprinkle powder, give a little something to everyone. French elites are fully aware of the great regressivity of their system of social security financing. But because of their heavy accent on employer contributions, the wide coverage of benefits, and the astonishing number of tiny privileges for various groups, the mass of people may have an illusion of equality. These tiny inspirational privileges are visible everywhere. Ride the Métro in Paris and you will see seats reserved by law for *mutilés de guerre*. Observe the washroom attendants or the keepers of state tobacco shops; they are typically the stern, black-clad widows of public servants, granted priority in such posts by a grateful state. And every working citizen receives a low-priced train ticket for his annual holiday.

To demonstrate whether working-class support for the welfare state rests more on the possibly mistaken perception of who gets what than on the actual incidence of taxes and benefits

67

would require comparison of pairs of countries contrasting sharply in regressivity of financing and progressivity of program emphasis. To these differences in net effects one could then relate mass surveys of attitudes about the welfare state and equality.

As I shall show in chapter 5, the prior task of discovering the real impact of all taxes and benefits considered together has barely begun, is enormously complicated, and is as yet available in usable form for only two countries, Britain and West Germany. And, as we have seen in chapter 2, directly relevant comparable surveys of public opinion have not yet begun.

In sum, among rich countries, the welfare state will be most developed and supporting welfare-state ideologies most powerful where a centralized government (1.1) is able to mobilize and must respond to a large, strongly organized working class (3.) with only modest rates of social (occupational and educational) mobility (2.1.1; 2.1.2); where the middle mass does not perceive its tax burden as grossly unfair relative to that of the rich and the upper middle class (2.1.3) and does not feel great social distance from the poor (2.1.4); and finally, where the tax system has low visibility (2.1.3), self-employment experience is meager (2.1.6), and the private welfare state limited (2.1.7).

4. The sources and effects of the welfare backlash.

Where social heterogeneity and internal cleavages are expressed in a decentralized polity (1.2.1); in a nation whose stratification system is characterized by a large middle mass, many opportunities for self-employment (2.1.6), for social mobility (2.1.1; 2.1.2), and for private health, welfare, and education benefits (2.1.7), and whose middle mass strongly feels the tax squeeze (2.1.3), then we should find such indicators of welfare backlash as the following:

- Taxpayer revolts
- White-collar and professional strikes designed to widen the income gap between high and low status occupations
- Political campaigns in which welfare-state issues are posed

68

- Moves to link benefits to earnings and set up tough eligibility requirements for flat benefits and in other ways prevent redistribution to the poor. Since there is a general tendency to loosen eligibility requirements and broaden coverage, the countries that swing slowly in that direction or stop moving may be seen as cases of hardened resistance.

A large, well-organized working class (3.) should reduce such tendencies.

To discover where resistance to the welfare state is hardening requires intensive field work and search for survey and other data. Although it will remain less systematic than analysis of data on public expenditures, such study of the incidence and roots of the welfare backlash is nevertheless crucial if we are to grasp the upper limits and programmatic thrust of the modern welfare state.

In such large variations in structure—in the centralization of government and the social heterogeneity of the population, in the shape of stratification and the opportunities and burdens of various strata and occupational groups; in the character and strength of the working class—we can find a powerful explanation for divergence in welfare-state development among rich countries, once they have established the programs common to all.

The Military, War, and
the Welfare State

Recently "radical sociology" (e.g., Gouldner, 1970) has revived the idea of Lasswell (1941) that modern society moves toward a "warfare-welfare" state in which political elites, alert to problems of national integration and morale, secure the collaboration of the masses for wars and disciplined sacrifice by extending social security, providing the symbols of participation, and an illusory equality. A second argument—this one a Marxist extension of Keynes—emphasizes the motives of political elites in adopting high levels of military spending, whatever the link between war and welfare. In order to avoid the deep depressions endemic to modern monopoly capitalism, it is said, these Western ruling classes are compelled to take up the slack with military spending; otherwise they would suffer economic stagnation and presumably political rebellion (Baran and Sweezy, 1966).

If the label "warfare-welfare" state or "garrison state" means anything, it has to mean a positive correlation between military expenditures and welfare expenditures. And if political elites in rich countries must invest heavily in the military to prevent economic stagnation, we should find that capitalist countries spend more of their resources on defense than noncapitalist countries at the same economic level, that the The Military, War, and the Welfare State most developed capitalist countries spend more on the military than the less developed capitalist countries, and finally, that the more of their resources the capitalist countries devote to the military the swifter their rate of economic growth and the lower their rate of unemployment.

A brief discussion of these complex relationships and the conditions under which they vary will shed light on the interplay of the welfare state, equality, and war. I shall argue (1) that, whatever positive connection there was between war and welfare in the past, modern conditions have made the two mutually subversive; and (2) that military spending in the richest countries dampens economic growth, has no necessary connection with unemployment rates, and has nothing to do with "capitalism."

BIG WARS AND LARGE-SCALE MOBILIZATION

The persuasive studies of Titmuss (1958), Briggs (1961), and others have taught us that World War II was oddly egalitarian. First, it brought full employment and capacity production, which meant a greater equalization of income. World War II saw blacks in America acquiring a foothold as semiskilled workers in urban industry. Many were upgraded in literacy and skill. The bars of discrimination began to weaken. Other minority groups, such as women, were integrated into the economy as they never had been before. Labor never had it so good.

Second, the argument of "equality of sacrifice" became irresistible. Why should some profiteer and others die? So the United States adopted excess profits taxes, steeper income taxes, rationing, wage-price controls with a massive enforcement machinery—the usual wartime arrangements to assure equality and stability. Such measures were not always successful, but on balance they added something to the thrust for equality. In Britain, the welfare state made great strides as Conservative

71

Party leaders pushed Labour Party programs. In 1940, only one child in thirty was fed at school; in 1945, it was one in three (Briggs, 1961, p. 226).

That big wars can foster equality is further evident in the American Civil War. Early on, the push for equality was quite limited. President Abraham Lincoln, in fact, advocated colonization of blacks and spurned the use of black volunteers. The wall of discrimination and prejudice against the freedmen of the North seemed impregnable. Irish mobs committed atrocities against blacks which in retrospect make contemporary race relations look tame. Using racial passions to stir up the masses, Democratic politicians scored gains in the 1862 congressional elections. But at the same time there were parades of departing black Union troops in northern cities and newspaper accounts of the battlefield performance of black troops in the South. White and black abolitionists kept up their steady pressure; foreign critics of slavery pressed their views. President Lincoln, facing battlefield reverses and manpower shortages, gradually reoriented his wartime policies, signaling the change by his Emancipation Proclamation. By the end of the war the Negro's legal position had markedly improved (Litwak, 1961).

Welfare developments of World War I in Britain (Hurwitz, 1949) and Germany (Feldman, 1966) confirm the general point: nations caught up in big wars, especially when they are losing battles and approaching total mobilization, find the political will to bring their official pronouncements and their public action closer together. If equality is official doctrine, some of their people will be made more equal.

Thus, the "guns-*and*-butter" argument is far from ludicrous. In fact, mobilization for war may be one of a larger class of national crises that inspire a collective willingness to move fast in the development of the welfare state (cf. Peacock and Wiseman, pp. xxiv–xxxi). If we examine the nine welfare-state leaders of table 2, only one, Sweden, escaped massive destruction or occupation or both in World War II. In contrast, of the nine countries at the bottom of welfare spending in that table, all but the USSR and Japan escaped such a crisis.

On closer inspection, Sweden may not be an exception to the hypothesis that deep crises promote equality. A systematic comparison of the pretax distribution of income in four European nations and the United States showed that in 1935 Sweden began with "the most unequal distribution of any we have recorded and wound up in 1954 with one of the least unequal" (Solow, 1960, pp. 113ff.). What triggered off this achievement in equality was the convergence in 1931–32 of a deepening depression, a nationwide protest over an incident in which government troops killed several striking sawmill workers and wounded many others, and a political scandal involving the corruption of Prime Minister Carl Ekman. These events constituted a national crisis which brought the Social Democrats and the Farmers' Party to power and cast the die for the accelerated development of the most celebrated welfare state of our time.[1]

Similarly, even the welfare-state laggards, when they have moved ahead at all, or have come close to moving, have done so when shaken by crisis. For example, from 1915 to 1918, as the United States approached World War I and finally entered it, a drive for universal compulsory health insurance was mounted from New York to California; sixteen states actually introduced such legislation; the American Medical Association, then under the control of academic physicians, was sympathetic; by 1918,

1. On May 13, 1931, at least four strikers at Ådalen were killed by troops protecting strikebreakers at the sawmills. This outrage inspired scattered demonstrations, the Communist establishment of a "Soviet Republic" at Ådalen, which actually ruled for a couple of weeks, a Social Democratic Party charge that the government was responsible for the murder of workers, and a huge labor demonstration in Stockholm. On March 12, 1932, while the Ådalen affair was still fresh in mass memory, the news broke that Ivar Kreuger, head of the Swedish Match Trust, had committed suicide after a desperate search for credit to sustain his financial empire. During the ensuing financial panic, investigation revealed that tycoon Kreuger had successfully bribed Prime Minister Ekman. An election of September 1932 brought a coalition of the Social Democrats and the Farmers' Party to power, led by the popular Per Albin Hansson. (Ander, 1958, pp. 165–170; Oakley, 1966, pp. 242–243.)

73

the country very nearly adopted national health insurance. The movement died in the quiet of the 1920s (cf. Anderson, 1972, pp. 64–73). Similarly, except for workmen's compensation, the United States did not join the general trend toward old-age pensions and unemployment insurance until the country reached the depths of the Great Depression, when President Franklin Roosevelt was able to put the Social Security Act on the books.

SMALL WARS AND LITTLE MOBILIZATION

As rich countries become richer and as international crises provoke the fear that war could become a nuclear holocaust, the probability of world war with massive mobilization decreases while the probability of limited war with small-scale, short-term, or no mobilization increases—as in the crises of French Indochina, Suez, Algeria, Vietnam, and the succession of short Arab-Israeli wars. The new technology has made the world "safe" for small wars.

Further, while the military budgets of most rich countries decrease as a fraction of GNP from 1950 to 1970 (see table 3), they remain high enough to serve as an added source of inflation and resource exhaustion, especially in countries at or near the center of alliances or regional blocs. The high military expenditures of the USSR, the United States, France, the United Kingdom, and Israel shown in table 3 reflect this new combination of high "peacetime" military budgets and small-to-medium-sized wars.

Does military spending undercut welfare spending? At first glance, and for cross-sectional data on many countries, military spending is irrelevant: In neither table 1 nor table 2 can any military influence on social security spending be detected. If we consider time-series data, however, and pinpoint the nations with the most bloated military budgets, the hypothesis that war and welfare have become mutually subversive receives support.

In the United States (1939–1968), France (1950–1965), and Britain (1947–1965) alike, defense spending has been negatively correlated with government spending for civilian needs—in order of negative effect, military spending undercuts welfare first, then education, then health (Russett, 1970, pp. 133, 137–156, 170–184). Further, the military spending is substantially independent of external military threats. In his study of expenditures from 1950 to 1962 among seven "communist" countries and seven "capitalist" countries, Pryor shows that the big determinant of defense spending (about half of the variance) is interaction between enemies—a mutually frantic escalation (Pryor, 1968, pp. 107–112ff.). The inflation of military budgets in the United States is evident in the "ratchet effect" (once you go up, as in World War I, World War II, and the Korean War, you do not revert to prewar levels, whatever the state of international tension). President Nixon's veto of a large education and health appropriation in 1970 is one of many slashes in civilian programs in response to military pressures (Russett, pp. 160, 175–177).

Preliminary analysis of the data in tables 2 and 3, presented graphically in figure 4, is consistent with these findings but adds insight into the lasting effects of a big peacetime military scare. Eliminating Israel as a special case, and concentrating on the sixteen countries for which we had complete trend data, this analysis underscores a crucial period in which military burdens in the rich countries have proved most costly to social security programs.

The beginnings of the cold war locate the most obvious, powerful, depressing effect of warfare on welfare. In those years of 1950–1952, the superpowers launched a nuclear arms race, developed rigid doctrines of international conspiracy and enemy encirclement, and demonstrated their willingness to be tough and take risks in such crises as Berlin and Korea. The resulting swift increase in military spending from 1950–1952 cast the die for a poor welfare performance for those countries most swept up in the crisis atmosphere. Thus, for the sixteen countries, great

75

TABLE 3: *Recent Trends in Military Spending as a Percent of GNP at Factor Cost for 22 Countries*

Country[a]	Social security as per-cent of GNP— 1960[b]	1950	1951	1952	1953	1954	1955	1956	1957	1958	1959	1960	1961	1962	1963	1964	1965	1966	1967	1968	1969	1970
Austria	21.0	0.8	1.0	0.6	0.6	0.1	0.2	1.0	1.5	1.6	1.6	1.3	1.3	1.4	1.4	1.8	1.4	1.5	1.5	1.5	1.5	1.3
Germany (FR)	19.6	5.2	6.0	6.5	5.0	4.7	4.8	4.2	4.8	3.4	5.1	4.7	4.7	5.6	5.9	5.3	5.0	4.7	5.0	4.1	3.9	3.7
Belgium	18.5	2.4	3.4	5.0	5.2	5.0	4.1	3.8	3.9	3.9	3.7	3.6	3.6	3.7	3.6	3.6	3.3	3.3	3.3	3.3	3.1	3.0
Netherlands	18.3	5.4	5.5	6.2	6.2	6.6	6.2	6.3	5.7	5.0	4.3	4.4	4.9	4.9	4.8	4.7	4.3	4.1	4.2	4.0	4.0	3.9
France	18.3	6.5	8.4	10.3	11.0	8.7	7.6	9.2	8.7	8.1	7.9	7.6	7.2	7.0	6.4	6.2	6.0	5.9	5.8	5.5	5.4	4.6
Sweden	17.5	4.1	4.2	4.7	5.3	5.3	5.2	5.1	5.0	5.1	5.0	4.8	4.7	5.0	5.0	4.9	4.6	4.4	4.2	4.1	4.2	3.9
Italy	17.5	4.6	5.1	5.5	4.6	4.9	4.5	4.5	4.3	4.3	4.2	4.0	3.5	3.5	3.7	3.7	3.7	3.8	3.5	3.3	3.0	3.0
Czechoslovakia	17.2	9.5	10.3	.....	8.0	7.2	.....	7.3	7.0	6.2	5.9	5.5	6.6	7.7	8.1	7.4	7.2	6.6	7.0	6.6	.....	.....
East Germany	16.4	.....	.....	.....	.....	.....	.....	.....	.....	2.4	.....	.....	1.6	4.1	4.2	4.1	4.5	4.5	4.9	7.9	.....	.....
United Kingdom	14.4	7.3	8.9	11.2	11.3	9.9	9.4	8.8	8.1	7.8	7.4	7.3	7.0	7.0	6.9	6.8	6.6	6.5	7.6	6.3	5.8	5.7
Denmark	13.9	1.8	2.3	3.0	3.7	3.6	3.6	3.4	3.5	3.3	2.9	3.1	2.9	3.4	3.5	3.3	3.2	3.1	3.4	3.3	3.0	2.8
Finland	13.1	2.1	2.2	1.5	1.7	1.6	1.8	1.7	1.7	1.8	2.0	1.9	2.0	2.8	2.1	1.6	1.9	1.8	2.3	2.2	1.6	1.5
Norway	12.6	2.6	3.4	4.5	5.7	5.7	4.4	3.9	4.0	4.0	4.1	3.6	3.7	4.0	4.0	3.9	4.2	4.0	3.9	4.2	4.0	4.0
New Zealand	11.8	1.5	2.3	3.1	3.3	2.8	2.5	2.5	2.4	2.3	2.3	2.4	2.0	1.8	1.7	1.9	2.1	2.2	2.2	2.2	1.9	2.1
Ireland	11.1	1.4	1.6	1.8	2.0	1.8	1.7	1.7	1.7	1.6	1.6	1.6	1.5	1.5	1.4	2.6	1.3	1.5	1.6	1.0	1.2	1.1
Canada	10.1	3.1	6.5	8.9	9.0	8.1	7.6	7.1	6.5	6.0	5.4	5.2	5.4	5.1	4.5	4.4	3.7	3.6	3.7	3.3	2.8	2.6
USSR[c]	10.1	.....	16.8	17.9	17.0	14.0	14.9	12.6	10.9	8.9	8.7	7.7	9.8	9.8	9.5	8.5	7.7	7.6	7.8	8.6	9.0	8.7

Switzerland	9.5	2.7	3.2	4.0	3.6	2.9	2.9	2.5	3.2	3.4	3.0	2.7	2.8	2.9	2.8	2.9	2.7	2.8	2.5	2.3	1.8	....
Australia	9.0	2.3	3.7	4.7	4.5	3.8	3.7	3.7	3.4	3.1	3.0	2.9	2.9	2.7	2.6	2.8	3.3	3.8	4.1	4.3	4.1	4.1
Israel	8.0	8.5	8.3	5.5	4.1	3.2	3.0	5.4	7.0	7.1	7.1	7.8	8.6	9.2	9.2	11.9	13.3	11.9	21.4	20.3	23.4	28.8
United States	7.9	5.4	10.9	14.9	14.8	12.9	11.1	10.7	10.9	11.0	10.3	9.9	9.9	10.1	9.6	8.7	8.2	9.1	10.2	10.1	9.4	8.7
Japan	6.2	....	0.7	1.0	0.9	1.0	1.1	1.1	1.0	1.1	1.1	1.1	1.0	1.0	0.8	1.1	1.0	1.0	0.9	0.9	0.8	0.8

[a] The source for military spending data for all nations except the USSR for the period 1950–1960 is the Stockholm International Peace Research Institute, *SIPRI Yearbook of World Armaments and Disarmaments, 1969/70* (Uppsala: 1970), pp. 259–281. For the USSR, data for the period 1951–1970 are taken from the Institute for Strategic Studies, *The Military Balance, 1972–1973* (London: 1972), p. 73. For all nations except the USSR, Australia, and New Zealand, spending data for the period 1961–1970 are taken from the U.S. Arms Control and Disarmament Agency, *World Military Expenditures, 1971* (Washington: 1972), pp. 18–21. For Australia and New Zealand, years 1961–1969, data are from the *SIPRI Yearbook*, for 1970, from *World Military Expenditures*. Definitions of military expenditures, as well as explanations of data selection and a discussion of the limits and uses of the data, are contained in the Appendix on Methods. Factor cost GNP is used instead of market price GNP to make more valid comparisons of countries that vary in their reliance on indirect taxes. See Appendix.

[b] Countries are ranked by social security spending as percent of GNP at factor cost for 1966. For further explanation of the social security spending data, see Appendix on Methods.

[c] See Appendix for discussion of estimates of Soviet military spending.

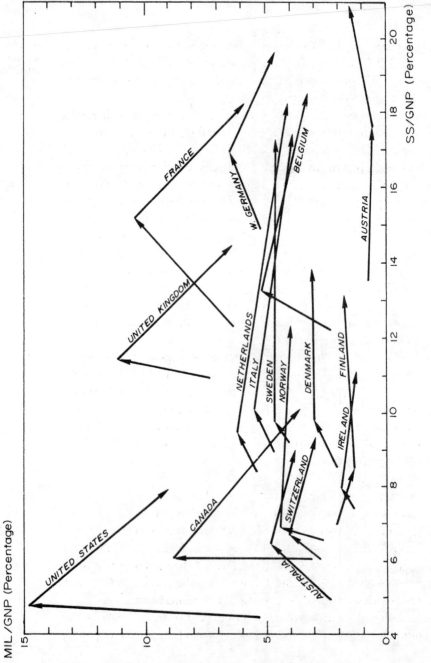

FIGURE 4. Relation of Trends in Military Effort to Trends in Social Security Effort, 1950–1952–1966: 16 Countries.

increases in military spending in 1950–1952 (military spend-
ing/GNP 1952 minus military spending/GNP 1950) are associated with small increases in social security spending for the
whole period 1950–1966 (r = − .43).

To illustrate these statistical patterns more concretely,
consider countries whose military spending was, on average, very
high in the early 1950s (USSR, U.S., U.K., Canada); they all
evidence practically no social security development in 1950–
1952 (in figure 4 the lines are almost vertical) and only slow
development thereafter. Contrast countries where military
spending was, on average, medium to low in the early 1950s:
from 1952 on, they typically stay steadily low in military
spending while they show sharp increases in social security effort
(Netherlands, Italy, Belgium, Sweden, and Norway).

The case of Israel is ambiguous. Because of three short wars
involving large-scale mobilization, the timing of changes in
Israeli welfare-warfare spending bears little relationship to the
cold war peaks and valleys of the countries included in figure 4.
Nevertheless, welfare and warfare in Israel appear to be antithet-
ical. When military spending as a proportion of GNP dropped
after the 1949 war, social security spending climbed. When
military effort during and after the 1956 war increased fivefold—
from 3 percent in 1955 to 14.2 percent in 1964—social security
effort remained almost static (6.2 percent to 6.9 percent). When
military spending dropped from 1964 to 1966, social security
effort again climbed.

Of course the welfare state marches on through thick and
thin; while acceleration of military spending can retard welfare
spending, it does not stop it. *All* countries increased social
security effort from 1950 to 1966 (see figure 4). What this
analysis of covariation in the two rates of change suggests is that,
at some level of abundance, a foreign policy accenting military
action without total and sustained mobilization is expensive
enough and inflationary enough to make the argument "cut the
domestic frills, balance the budget" seductive. But it is not so

79

expensive as to put the middle majority in the mood for "equality of sacrifice." Thus we see no push for redistributional welfare programs comparable to the surge of World War II.

In considering the effect of big military budgets and little wars on equality we must not assume a simple diversion of money from health and welfare to what is loosely called "defense," although that is part of the story. I have come instead to this formulation of the problem:

5. Under conditions of little mobilization,

Heavy military burdens ⎯⎯→ political energy and expert talent drained away from domestic programs, economic resources used up ⎯⎯→ gap between official ideology (talk of equality and higher living standards) and practice grows wider ⎯⎯→ disaffection of poor and minorities and welfare backlash among middle mass ⎯⎯→ slowdown in welfare-state development. (This hypothesis is elaborated in Wilensky, 1972.)

THE CITIZENS' ARMY AND THE WELFARE STATE

A problem untouched by research, which requires an historical analysis of the origins of the welfare state going beyond the economic and demographic mainsprings discussed in chapter 2, is the effect of mass conscription on welfare-state development.

On the one hand, when the institution of the citizen army emerged in modern Europe it forced the spread of many rights and benefits to potential conscripts—especially among the lower classes, whose loyalty had to be assured. Conscription, at least in the early stages, was egalitarian in effect (cf. Andreski, 1968, 2nd ed., pp. 68ff.). On the other hand, in contemporary rich countries conscription may have mixed effects. By increasing direct military influence on public expenditures, conscription may undermine the capacity of elites to respond to the push for equality. The argument is complex. First, the citizens' army, because it is cheap, facilitates upward pressures on military manpower; volunteers, or mercenaries, because they are very expensive, put a brake on expansion of military manpower. Second, military bases become political constituencies. The chief political influence of the military establishment in the United States rests not directly upon contracts (weapons systems, etc.), which are feast-and-famine benefits for a few areas and special industries, but upon bases and manpower, which are steady sources of community income and are more widely dispersed (Russett, 1970). Seattle cannot count on Boeing and bombers; San Antonio is secure with its big army and air force bases. Thus I arrive at the following hypothesis:

5.1. *In decentralized polities conscription increases the resistance to reallocation of military spending to the welfare state among the publics who benefit from stable military installations and among legislators who represent these publics.*

In exploring this hypothesis, the social historian has to solve several difficult problems. First, how far back must we go to search for events that allegedly cast the die for equality? The initiation of conscription may create a political climate for launching welfare programs but have little influence on levels and types of public spending a century later. Second, how do we distinguish (1) nations at the minimum economic level required to institute mass conscription and to field a large army, from (2) nations that can support large armies because of the mixed blessing of dependence on outside military aid through location at or near the center of a pact or alliance run by a big power? On the expense of the standing army, Adam Smith once estimated that "among the civilized nations of modern Europe . . . not more than one hundredth part of the inhabitants of any country can be employed as soldiers, without ruin to the country which pays the expence of their service" (Adam Smith, [5th ed., 1789], 1937, pp. 657–658). By the 1960s the United States, like other world powers, had exceeded Smith's cautious formula and provoked the spread of popular pacifism. But in tables 1 and 4 we can see that poor countries, too, can be lavish in the support of a military establishment. In 1966, among the poorest half of those sixty-four countries, five spent at least 6 percent of their limited resources on the military: Taiwan, 13 percent; Iraq, 11; Syria, 10; Burma, 7; Portugal, 6. Such nations, of course, can field large armies in part because of the dedicated support of rich patrons; four have been heavily dependent on one of the two superpowers; Burma has depended on arms from both sides. Although agencies that estimate military expenditures try to exclude military aid from the military budgets of recipient nations, it is likely that, in fact, some of the aid shows up in the expenditure figures of tables 1 and 4, so these figures reflect an interaction between internal and external eagerness to devote resources to the military. Because of their low level of development as well as these ambiguities in the data, we cannot yet know the effect of such resource allocation when and if the militant poor countries become rich enough to develop a functioning welfare state. Neither can we know the implications of an oil-sellers' cartel for the capacity of poor countries of the Middle East, newly loaded with cash, to indulge in a huge military establishment, whatever their state of welfare.

Finally, in several rich countries, the citizens' army is now being replaced by smaller, specialized, volunteer forces. Whatever effect the end of mass conscription may have on the chances of military coups d'état, it may decrease the influence of citizens who make a living from large army bases. That conscription is going out of fashion may thereby indirectly release resources for welfare spending, at least in countries responsive to local popular pressures.

MILITARY SPENDING, CAPITALISM, UNEMPLOYMENT, AND GROWTH RATES

We have already seen that, contrary to the Marxian argument, the prosperity of rich "capitalist" countries in the period after World War II is not rooted in military spending. For the cross section of sixty-four countries listed in table 4 military spending as a fraction of GNP is uncorrelated with either type of political system or level of economic development (see Appendix). Consistent with the findings of Pryor (1968), Russett (1970), and Szymanski (1973), table 3 shows further that from 1961 to 1968 (years for which we have no missing data) military spending as a proportion of GNP averaged 7.0 percent for the three richest communist countries (Czechoslovakia, East Germany, and the USSR); 5.0 percent for the fourteen richest aligned "capitalist" countries; and 2.4 percent for the five capitalist neutrals (Sweden, Switzerland, Austria, Finland, and Ireland). If we match capitalist and communist countries by alliance or pact position, or economic level, no significant difference in military effort can be detected (see also the path diagrams, figs. 1, 2, and 3, chapter 2).

As for the idea that military spending is a major device of a capitalist ruling class to avoid a repetition of the Great Depression of the 1930s, Szymanski (1973) casts doubt on that argument in his study of the eighteen capitalist nations of greatest wealth in 1968, which are identical to the countries listed in tables 2 and 3 except for my inclusion of Ireland. Controlling for GNP per capita and for size of the economy, Szymanski shows (1) that for both 1950–1968 and 1960–1968, countries with the highest military effort were growing more slowly than those with lower military/GNP ratios; and (2) that among the six largest capitalist powers (United States, Japan, West Germany, France, Great Britain, Italy), those with the heaviest military burdens have been greatly hindered in their economic growth by their military effort, while military spending in the twelve less rich countries has on average enhanced their growth rates slightly. In general, the evidence suggests that if capitalist elites are using military spending and expansionism to avoid economic stagnation, they are deluding themselves; the strategy, if it is one, is self-defeating.

Since I have suggested that, under conditions of massive and sustained mobilization, military effort may lower unemployment rates and thereby increase equality, special attention should be given to the effect of the cold war and related small wars on employment levels since 1950, a period when mobilization has remained limited in every rich country but Israel. Consistent with Baran and Sweezy and John Maynard Keynes alike, Szymanski shows that the higher the level of *total* government spending, the lower the level of unemployment (average rates of 1964–1968) and the higher the rate of growth in GNP per capita (1950–1968 and 1960–1968). When we sort out the effects of military from nonmilitary spending, however, we see a more complicated picture. Military expenditures reduce unemployment a bit more than do nonmilitary expenditures (Szymanski, pp. 6–7). But among welfare-state laggards (countries with low nonmilitary expenditures such as the United States, Canada, Switzerland, Australia, Japan), those with the greatest military expenditures have the highest unemployment rates—a finding that also holds for the six biggest capitalist countries (pp. 8–9). Only among welfare-state leaders or middle-rank spenders (countries with high nonmilitary spending such as Sweden, Norway, France, the Netherlands, West Germany, Austria, Denmark, Italy) and among lesser capitalist powers does military spending appear to reduce unemployment rates (p. 9). In other words, if you are already spending a lot on public civilian purposes, to throw in an extra effort on external security will help reduce unemployment slightly—an average of 0.6 percent (p. 9). But if you are already a big military spender, to hold back on public civilian expenditures will *increase* unemployment substantially—an average of 1.2 percent (p. 14). In short, where the welfare state is poorly developed, under modern conditions military spending diverts skilled manpower and scarce funds away from productive employment and thereby slows down economic growth and worsens unemployment (cf. Melman, 1965).

Summary. We need more intensive analysis of the fate of welfare programs under varying conditions of mass mobilization, mass conscription, and war. Thus far, there is no evidence of the

84

emergence of a warfare-welfare state. The great powers will never again match their previous performance where the destruction of world war brought the spread of social rights and benefits. The only equality resulting from a new world war would be the equality of the grave.

5

The Impact of the Welfare State
on Real Welfare

The welfare state is a major structural tendency of modern society. With economic growth all countries develop similar social security programs. Whatever their economic or political system, whatever the ideologies of elites or masses, the rich countries converge in types of health and welfare programs, in increasingly comprehensive coverage, and, to a lesser extent, in methods of financing. The fraction of national resources devoted to these programs climbs, eventually at a decelerating rate. Although the root cause of the general trend is economic growth and its demographic and bureaucratic outcomes, at an advanced stage of affluence we find momentous differences in the size and strength of national commitments to the welfare state, in program emphasis, in the politics of welfare, and, of course, in administrative style—how efficient or sloppy, how tough or indulgent, how mean or generous.

Earlier chapters have concentrated on explaining why political elites allocate various proportions of their nation's resources to social security. But what are the results of all this welfare effort for equality, health, and economic and psychological security? What does the welfare state do for real welfare?

Speculation informed by illustrative evidence of varied quality is the best that can be offered. To guide such speculation we must distinguish between economic effects, where the data are best, and noneconomic effects, where data are typically weak or nonexistent; and we must note the difference between the short run, where some effects can be traced, and the long run, in which we will not only all be dead but which must be left to futurologists and other prophets.

EFFECTS ON INCOME DISTRIBUTION

I began with the statement that the net effect of the welfare state is egalitarian. In financing, most welfare and health programs are probably regressive, but in payout they may be on the whole progressive (cf. Wilensky, 1965, pp. xiii–xvi; Pryor, 1968, pp. 302ff.). In some circles these are fighting words. Income distribution is a classic problem which connects basic social-science research with recurrent issues of political combat. In every rich democracy the problem of taxes and spending as they affect equality and social justice has surfaced as a hot political issue. The slower growth rates of the mid-seventies intensified these debates by exacerbating and publicizing pre-existing inequities.

Although the following discussion paints a slightly rosy picture, which "radicals" might label a defense of the status quo, I do not try to specify what a good income distribution is. (I do favor a greater shift of resources to the less privileged portions of the population than is typical of the welfare-state laggards, if we recognize that the least privileged—unpopular deviants, handicapped people, racial minorities, single parents, workers in dangerous trades—are not always poor.) Instead, I aim to specify the gaps in evidence and to sketch the outlines of a more intelligent debate about the distributional effects of the welfare state.

There are many ways of describing a country's income distribution. Much futile controversy arises when politically important assertions and counter assertions are made about "the" distribution of income when differences in research procedures explain most of the differences in dispute. Differences in method include the use of different recipient units, definitions and sources of income, periods over which income is accumulated, levels of aggregation, positions within the distribution to be compared, dates chosen for comparison.[1] Pessimists and optimists, egalitarians and antiegalitarians, too often select procedures that will sustain their preconceptions about the main drift.

Among the major questions in any analysis of income distribution are the following: (1) What share of national personal income do the very richest families take? (2) What proportion of all the families and unattached individuals (persons not living with relatives) falls in different income brackets in different years? (3) How fast does the purchasing power of various strata go up or down? (4) What are the net effects on income distribution of taxes and public consumption expenditures? All these questions are part of the very broad problem of distributive justice, but I shall ignore the share of national income taken by the very richest families and concen-

1. In the literature on the shape of modern society, the area of income distribution is not only intensely controversial; it also has a weak data base. In household surveys, people lie more about income than any other topic; sophisticated survey researchers have been forced to devote much attention to breaking through this barrier. In discussions of income distribution by social scientists and journalists alike, the size of income shares and assertions about trends depend upon the *recipient unit* used (individual, family, consumer-spending unit, household, head of household, other); the *sources and definition of income* (do the data include wages and salaries, capital gains, expense accounts, income in kind such as free schools or health services, transfer payments such as pensions, income before taxes or after taxes?); the *period over which income is cumulated* (hourly rates, hourly earnings, weekly or monthly salaries or earnings; yearly income or averages of several years); the *levels of aggregation* (shares of the upper 1 percent, 5 percent, deciles, quintiles, or whatever, and, when the data are cut finely, there is the added problem of how much sampling error is increased for the extremes of the distribution); *what parts of the distribution are compared* (e.g., distance between deciles one and ten versus that between decile one and the median income); *the dates chosen for comparison* (for U.S. data, to capture the main drift toward equality, look at long time periods; to show the reverse, focus on an appropriate short period, such as the 1950s). (Cf. Kuznets, 1950, 1953; Wilensky and Lebeaux, 1958, pp. 84–85, 100–106.)

trate only on the last question of income distribution, in itself
complicated enough.

If by distributive justice we mean the guarantee of a socially
defined minimum standard of living for everyone, whatever his
or her current or past contribution to the economy, then this
entire book has focused on distributive justice and the associated problem of income distribution. If by distributive justice
we mean popular consensus about (1) equal pay for equal work
and (2) the content of jobs as related to job rewards (unequal
pay for unequal skills and job demands), then the "unearned"
income of the idle rich is momentous; a clipper of coupons
should not receive a hundred times what a coal-miner earns.
Important as this problem is, sociologically and philosophically,
it is irrelevant in the present context; it is not a major problem
of income redistribution. For dividing up the income of the
richest 1 percent or 2 percent or 5 percent of the population—
idle and nonidle alike—among the rest of the population would
add little to any one family's income; indeed, even dividing it
among the lowest fifth would not do much for families in that
bracket. Any effective redistribution of income must take
substantial amounts away from a much larger population than
critics of income inequality usually have in mind.

My account of the distributional impact of the welfare
state also ignores the disguised privileges of the rich simply
because adequate data are unavailable; for instance, neither of
the two relevant studies of taxes and benefits—one for England,
the other for Germany—include expense accounts or capital
gains. Both are important chunks of top-bracket incomes.
Expense accounts are not taxed at all, though they clearly
become part of the standard of living of high-level business,
professional, and sales people. Capital gains are taxed at a lower
rate than ordinary income; in effect they offer a real tax
advantage for those who have large sums available to invest in
real estate, stocks, and so forth, which may yield both income
now and a lightly taxed capital gain later. The rich can
sometimes avoid a capital gains tax—simply by retaining their

investments until death, at which time their offspring may enjoy a more advantageous tax basis (as in the U.S.) or avoid death duties by giving wealth away to their offspring a legally specified number of years before death (as in the U.K.).

Even without these corrections, the data show that the rich are hardly being squeezed to the wall by the welfare state; their situation is very likely even better than these studies suggest. My aim, however, is to estimate the impact of the welfare state on the income of the poor in relation to the upper half to three-quarters of the income distribution. In other words, do health and welfare programs improve the income of the lowest fifth or lowest quarter in relation to the middle majority and, indeed, considerable parts of the nonrich upper middle class?

Short-run Equality. If we consider only the short run—all of the transactions between people with different incomes at one time—and take account of the social composition of the poor, the case is obvious. The aged are a large fraction of the poor; much of social insurance goes to them, as we have seen from the great power of the fraction of aged as a predictor of welfare spending (figs. 1, 2, and 3). The aged and the poor are more often sick; they receive a disproportionate share of public expenditures on health. Large families and women heading broken homes are overrepresented among the poor; family allowances and public assistance go disproportionately to them. For the time of their travail, the unemployed and job-injured are concentrated among low-income families; again the payout is progressive. Even veterans' benefits—which in the United States constitute the only welfare program with generous federal standards and financing—are redistributive because the benefits flow to the indigent and the working class, who are heavily overrepresented among veterans and "war victims" (e.g., veterans' widows and children).

Does inflation negate the redistributive effect of welfare spending? At first glance, inflation erodes benefits; without cost-of-living escalators, the aged and other beneficiaries living on fixed incomes suffer. But in fact some benefits in some countries are tied to cost-of-living escalators; for instance, since 1968 monthly pensions in Canada have been automatically adjusted for changes in the Canadian consumer price index. Austria, Denmark, Sweden, Finland, Belgium, France, the Netherlands, Israel, and Italy have also linked pension benefits to wage or price indexes or both. With or without such arrangements, welfare and health expenditures are rising faster than GNP in most rich countries (OECD, 1972). Further, if the system has a large earnings-related element in its financing, more people pay more social insurance taxes as their money incomes climb—especially if the state has set the income ceiling for calculation of insurance contributions high. Since the payout is typically more progressive than the financing is regressive, the downward redistribution may actually be enhanced by inflation.

Even in the obvious case of the short run there are some complexities, although they are not fatal to the argument of egalitarian payout. For instance, recent increases in old-age pensions in the United States have paradoxically increased the number of old people enumerated as "poor" in our surveys of low-income families. The reason: squeezed to the wall financially, many aged Americans have been forced to double up with their working children or other relatives and have thereby been counted as above the poverty line, along with the family on which they were reluctantly dependent. When such dependent aged receive even small increases in real social security benefits, they move out on their own, choosing a more independent life—and then appear in the statistics on family poverty (cf. Murray, 1971; or Orshansky, 1965*a* and 1965*b*). But these complexities are merely statistical illusions, reflecting the limits of concepts and measures of poverty.

If the short-run progressive payout of the welfare state were offset or overwhelmed by extremely regressive financing, the case I am arguing would be weak. What evidence we have, however, suggests that the payout is overwhelmingly progressive while the financing is only mildly regressive, with a net balance clearly favoring the poor. Although some research has been done in Germany and Norway (United Nations, Economic Commission for Europe, 1967b), the most solid, thorough study of the incidence of both government taxes and government benefits published as yet for any country is based on the annual Family Expenditure Survey conducted since 1957 by the British Department of Employment and analyzed by the Central Statistical Office, the Department of Health and Social Security, and other government departments.[2] Let us focus on data for the year 1970.

That indirect taxes are regressive is part of the folklore of social criticism. The increased reliance on such taxes—the sales taxes, the value-added tax, and "luxury" taxes on such poor

2. This sample survey of about 3,200 British households each year through 1966 and 7,000 from then on was used primarily to prepare a consumer price index but has achieved multiple uses. The topics covered include what the respondent families paid in direct taxes and social security contributions and what they received in benefits. In addition, the incidence of indirect taxes is imputed to households of different size and income level on the basis of their observed patterns of spending on products taxed at different rates.

The analysts go to heroic lengths to improve the validity of their estimates. For instance, they adjust upward their estimates of indirect taxes on products such as liquor, tobacco, and ice cream, which survey respondents underreport in relation to the sales volume known from actual collection of excise and sales taxes. Employee contributions to social security are counted as direct taxes; employer contributions, as indirect taxes which are assumed to raise the price of their products. This procedure yields a slightly lower regressivity of social security contributions than if we counted both employee and employer contributions as a direct tax on the employee, but should make only a very small difference in the incidence of all taxes combined. Estimates of benefits include not only the cash receipts from pensions, family allowances, social assistance, rent rebates, and other welfare benefits, but also a rough allocation of the value of free schools and health care to the beneficiary households. In principle, even such important components of income as investment income and tax refunds on mortgage interest are included, although, in practice, they are perhaps underreported. Income-survey experience suggests, however, that through sample bias and respondent resistance alike, *both* extremes of the distribution are underreported, so that welfare payments and similar transfers are understated, too. I would guess that the picture of income distribution below is little affected by these variations in survey efficiency in this unusually effective survey. The survey is reported in United Kingdom, *Economic Trends* (annually).

92

man's luxuries as beer and tobacco—certainly gives little comfort to those who cherish equality. Pessimism, however, may be
unwarranted. If we examine the incidence of particular regressive taxes in isolation not only from all other taxes but from
social security and other benefits in cash and kind—in other
words if, when we divide taxes by household income, we ignore
all sources of income other than current earnings—we will
produce highly pessimistic and highly misleading statistics. The
British data are detailed enough to permit this exercise. Indirect
taxes, the notorious threat to equality, are bizarrely regressive if
we calculate their impact as a fraction of original incomes: they
take 175 percent of the poorest households' incomes (whose
original incomes—before they receive any welfare benefits—are
less than £260 per year) and only 17 percent of the richest
households' income (original incomes over £3,104 per year)
(calculated from Central Statistical Office, 1972, Appendix II,
table 1, p. xxi). If instead we calculate the incidence of indirect
taxes as a fraction of original-income-plus-cash-benefits (pensions, unemployment compensation, family allowances, etc.),
then indirect taxes are much less regressive: the range shrinks to
25 percent of the lowest incomes, to 16 percent of the highest
(calculated from ibid.).

Direct taxes, on the other hand, are distinctly progressive:
the poorest households paid virtually none in 1970, and the
percentage of original-income-plus-cash-benefits taken by direct
taxes rose evenly through fifteen income brackets to 22 percent
among the richest group (calculated from table F, p. xii). If we
look at all taxes together, we see a mild progression from 25
percent of the poorest households' original-incomes-plus-cash-
benefits to 38 percent for the richest.

Supporting my argument about the highly progressive
payout of the welfare state, total benefits progress uniformly
from a mere 8 percent of the original-income-plus-cash-benefits
of the rich to 114 percent for the poor (table D, p. ix).

Finally, and most important, is the clearly progressive
pattern we uncover when we take account of all taxes and all

benefits and income at once, including the value of health services and schooling. Household income after *all* taxes and benefits in 1970 ranged from 726 percent of original income for the poorest households to 70 percent of original income for the richest households—moving through a steady gradient over the fifteen income brackets (table A, p. vi). In other words, taxes and benefits taken together have a *highly* egalitarian effect on income distribution.

Because comparable data are available for so short a period I have so far said nothing about trends. Nevertheless, a British expert on income distribution has attempted to analyze these data from 1961 through 1971 (Nicholson, 1974, pp. 71–91). After adjusting the figures for some definitional changes, which chiefly affect national insurance contributions, and taking careful account of other possible biases, Nicholson concludes that there was "remarkable stability" in the degree of inequality in final income during that decade. A slight increase in inequality of original income was offset by an increase in progressivity of the net effect of all taxes and benefits. Thus, the inequality produced by rising unemployment and other forces in the 1960s was offset by the redistributional effects of the welfare state. That is something Prime Minister Harold Wilson, whose back was to the wall in 1970, could have claimed as his very own, since the main source of that uphill achievement was improvements the Labour government made in National Insurance and Supplementary Benefits in 1965 and subsequently; but the data, once again, did not catch up with the political actors.

That the best detailed data demonstrating the short-run egalitarian impact of the welfare state are from Britain may be a good clue to the general situation of rich countries. Britain is fourteenth in per capita income among our twenty-two; and it is neither a welfare-state leader nor a laggard. This is not to say that rich countries are uniform in the net redistributive effects of taxes and welfare spending; in the absence of comparable national household surveys we cannot know. It is to say that if both affluence and the welfare state at this middling British level are egalitarian, the effects of more welfare spending in richer countries are unlikely to be inegalitarian—again, in the short run and despite the obvious variations in patterns of taxing, contributions, and benefits (see chapter 3).

A German estimate of net effects of taxes and benefits (1955 and 1960) is the only other national study that is similar in concept to the British surveys, although somewhat different in method. It makes no attempt to allocate benefits in kind (18 percent of total German benefits in 1960). Nevertheless it roughly confirms the interpretation that in the short run the welfare state redistributes income to the poor.[3]

Long-run Question Marks. While informed statements about the short-run effects of the welfare state on income distribution are thus beginning to be possible, assertions about the long-run impact remain highly speculative. Consider the outcome of a large-scale national health service like that of Britain. There is

3. Schmidt, Schwarz, and Thiebach, *Die Umverteilung des Volkseinkommens in der Bundesrepublik Deutschland 1955 und 1960*, Tübingen 1965, as cited in United Nations, Economic Commission for Europe, 1967b. All the following statements refer to table 6.17, ch. 6, p. 31. Total taxes were highly regressive (and indirect taxes were even worse) when their incidence was calculated as a fraction of original income. When we recalculate them as a fraction of original-income-plus-cash-benefits, total taxes become mildly progressive, rising from 20 percent for the poorest (original incomes less than DM 1,200 a year) through ten income groups to peak at 37 percent (DM 12,000–15,000 a year) and taper off over the three richest groups to 33 percent for original incomes over DM 24,000 a year. Benefits, as in Britain, were highly progressive even though benefits in kind were omitted: from 4 percent of the original incomes of the top groups to 748 percent for the lowest, or from 4 percent to 88 percent of original-income-plus-cash-benefits. Taxes and (cash) benefits taken together were strongly redistributional: the net gain to the poorest households was 576 percent of their original incomes; the net cost to the richest, 31 percent. It should be noted that redistribution only affected the position of the poorest quartile compared with the rest of the nation: for more affluent citizens with original incomes over DM 6,000 a year, the range of net loss (taxes minus benefits) was only from 27.7 percent to 31.4 percent of original incomes. That the German system is somewhat less progressive than that of the United Kingdom may reflect the heavier German reliance on earnings-related contributions and benefits in their pension schemes and the meager development of social assistance for the poor (what the Germans call "social help").

some direct evidence that the National Health Service is used most intensively by the least well off—the old, the young, the poor, the single (Rein, 1969)—although they do not tend to receive the highest quality service (Klein, 1973). If, however, every other force making for the superior health of the upper half of the education and income distribution is not simultaneously equalized, the long-run effect of public health expenditures may be highly regressive. The poor die young—before they can contract the chronic diseases that dearly cost national health schemes. The more affluent citizens live to a riper age, chronically collecting health services paid for by the lifelong taxes of the deceased poor. A program that is highly progressive at a cross-sectional moment may be highly regressive in the lifetime of particular generations.

NONECONOMIC EFFECTS

Any evaluation of the noneconomic effects of health and welfare programs for either the long run or the short is extremely difficult. One stimulus for the "social indicators" (or social reporting) movement (Duncan, 1969) has been the vacuum in which discussion of the effects of social policy proceeds—often a total absence of relevant data. To fill that vacuum sociologists and policy makers alike have been attracted to—some would say mesmerized by—the idea that we can construct some system of social accounts comparable to the economists' national income and product accounts; or, more broadly, that we can devise measures of social change for use in understanding social policy effects over time in one country and eventually in many.

Can Appropriate "Social Indicators" Be Developed? Aside from measures of the effects of taxes and benefits on income distribution discussed above, the list of possible indicators of the social and economic effects of the welfare state is long. Although I am not convinced that such lists and the data-gathering they imply will soon prove fruitful, I have constructed one to illustrate the enormous research tasks involved. I have grouped a few typical indicators of real welfare by major types of public expenditure, recognizing that a program "input" in one area (e.g., school resources devoted to showing students that smoking is harmful) may be an "output" in another area (reduced rates of lung cancer), and therefore the conventional distinctions between, say, education and health are at times artificial. I shall later show why many of these apparently valid indicators of welfare are, on closer inspection, of only modest utility.

1. Impact of welfare and health spending on welfare and equality. National variations in such indicators as the following:
   - Age-specific mortality rates
   - Disease rates by occupation or educational stratum
   - Other measures of the efficacy of medical-care delivery systems
   - Fertility rates (on assumption that the higher they are the worse for welfare)
   - Average family size by stratum
   - Unemployment rates (total and by stratum). Other dependency rates
   - Earnings replacement rate of unemployment insurance
   - Earnings replacement rate of pensions
   - Income of aged as deviation from median family income
   - Average age of retirement; percentage of older categories in retirement; opportunities for part-time work for the aged
   - Attitudes toward or concern with health and medical care; economic insecurity, old age; equality, the poor, minorities
2. Impact of education expenditures on welfare and equality. National variations in such indicators as the following:
   - Enrollment rate of relevant age-grade in colleges and universities; in all schools; in nurseries
   - Enrollment rates by occupation or education of parents
   - Teacher/student ratios
   - Spending per student on books and supplies
   - Teacher pay relative to that of other professionals
   - Student and teacher performance measures
   - Attitudes toward and concern with educational opportunity for self and children; quality of education; crisis of higher education; youth cultures
3. Impact of housing expenditures on welfare and equality. National variations in the following:
   - Investment in housing per capita

- Number of dwellings per 1,000 population
- Number of rooms per 1,000 population
- Percentage of dwellings with lavatory; with bathtubs, showers; with electricity
- Above rates by occupational and educational stratum
- Attitudes toward and concern with housing, the urban environment

4. Miscellaneous measures of equality, especially by descent (race, ethnicity, and religion), age, and sex. National variations in the following:
    - Position of minorities (including "guest workers" in such places as Switzerland and West Germany)
    - Position of the aged (see above)
    - Position of women—e.g., women as a percentage of the nonagricultural labor force; high status jobs; positions of great authority. Percentage of married women working; opportunities for part-time work; provisions for child care, and so forth

5. Miscellaneous measures of safety, such as the incidence of victimization by criminal acts, and risks of death by war. National variations in attitudes toward such risks.

At first glance such indicators of real welfare have an appearance of solidity. We would perhaps be in a better position to assess alternative social policies if for each of them we had reliable, valid data comparable over time and nations. But I am skeptical about the immediate prospects of obtaining comparable data. Further, if social indicators or measures of social trends are unguided by precise theoretical or practical purposes, they will not exceed the limited utility of omnibus national censuses. The kinds of intensive cross-national studies necessary to estimate the real output of public consumption expenditures (or, for that matter, private expenditures) have barely begun. The best of them remind us of the complexities of measurement and evaluation implied by lists of social indicators.

Health Care versus Real Health: Why Skepticism Is Appropriate. A model for the painstaking studies required to develop sensible social indicators is Anderson's comparison of health care in the United States, Sweden, and England (1972). Although some informed speculation is possible, the conclusions offer slim hope that we will soon know the real output of health and welfare programs. Even such simple statistics as age-specific mortality rates—an indicator of the opportunity for life itself—turn out to be impossible to link to any particular health policy.

An intensive examination of expenditures, organization, and performance in the three countries from 1950 to 1970 led Anderson to one reluctant conclusion after another: the possibilities for rational planning of health services are restricted because we lack adequate concepts and measures of health itself, let alone of the cost-effectiveness of various kinds of care. Physical health aside, there are not even comparative data on the satisfaction or comfort of patients in different countries. Insofar as rates of physical changes—morbidity, disability, and mortality—are comparable, they are very difficult to interpret and even more difficult to link to any specific aspect of health-care spending, organization, or delivery.

For instance, morbidity and disability rates tend to be inversely related to mortality rates: ". . . strenuous efforts to save babies born with serious congenital defects will decrease the infant mortality rate while at the same time increasing the morbidity and disability rates for young children" (Anderson, p. 147). One indicator of health performance often cancels out another—a barrier which we can surmount by striking a net balance of effects.

A more serious problem of interpretation is the multiple causation of any health output we can measure. Sweden's celebrated infant-mortality rate, for example, is much lower than that of England and the United States. Further, its age-specific mortality rates are slightly lower at nearly every age level. Finally, by the measure of age-specific mortality rates up to age sixty-five, Sweden's general performance is better than that of the two best-performing states of the United States—Hawaii and Utah—and it is also better than that of Minnesota, a state

99

similar to Sweden in climate, economy, and population (p. 158). But how much of this superior performance can be explained by Sweden's health-care system, how much by liberal abortion laws that encourage termination of high-risk pregnancies, and how much by other social policies, such as health-relevant programs in nutrition, education, and housing?

Similarly, consider the superior performance of the United States in mortality rates for those aged seventy-five and over. One explanation could be that the United States concentrates its health-care system on the elderly, while the British and Swedish systems concentrate on children. But it is equally plausible and equally true that the United States does poorly with health and mortality under age one and in middle adulthood, and therefore its low old-age mortality is caused less by the geriatric style of American medicine and more by the Darwinian survival of the fittest: American citizens who manage to live past seventy-five are a healthy and tenacious lot (Anderson, p. 150). The last explanation is consistent with the very high early mortality rates and very low mortality rates over sixty-five of American blacks and the citizens of Albania and Greece.

Further complicating the picture are the clear contrasts between the systems of medical care in the three countries Anderson examines (pp. 115–160). System contrasts in "input" are evidently not connected in any direct way to any measurable output. If we include public and private sectors, health expenditures in relation to gross national income in 1950 were about the same in the United States (5.3 percent) and England (5.4), yet quite low in Sweden (3.2), the best performer in mortality rates. By 1968 Sweden had become the top spender (8.1 percent), with the United States a close second (7.5) and Britain, home of the most socialized system of all, cut down to the bottom in cost (5.2). What did the money buy? Comparing the United States and Sweden, the Swedes use hospitals much more, public health nurses and nurse-midwives much more, and physicians much less than do the Americans.[4] It is fair to say that the United States is doctor rich (and has rich doctors); it has an abundance of specialists and a superabundance of surgeons. The connection of these system differences with Sweden's lower mortality rates are not obvious, unless one wishes to argue that a big supply of physicians, practicing mainly in private offices, increases the death rate.

Anderson abandons the attempt to link attributes of the system of medical care to customary indices of health and, in the end, argues that the main thing we can say with assurance is that Sweden is much superior to the United States in *equality of access* to doctors, dentists, drugs, and other medical facilities and personnel—whatever such equal access may mean for health—and that illness is more of a threat to family solvency in the United States. Although the British data on differences in access to medical facilities by income are somewhat fragmentary, the British appear to be like the Swedes in equality of dignified access to physicians.

Even these findings are not trivial. The unhappy combination of very high infant mortality rates in the United States and a rate of improvement slower than that of Sweden may not be entirely explained by the inequities in access to medical care in the United States, or the American tendency to invest in the chronic ailments of the affluent aged. Nevertheless, such differences in the organization, quality, and distribution of medical care reinforce the other differences we have uncovered in our comparison of welfare-state leaders and laggards. Sweden, like

4. Anderson (1972, pp. 121–140) reports the following data (for 1967 unless otherwise indicated):

	Physicians per 100,000 population	Average no. physician visits per year	Hospital as primary site of physicians providing patient care	General hospital days per 1,000 pop.	Hospital beds per 1,000 pop., 1968
U.S.	158	4.3	24%	2.5	8.3
Sweden	117	2.5	64%	5.0	16.3
England	119	5.9	51%	3.0	9.6

some of the other countries at the top of our list of twenty-two, not only distributes medical care more aggressively and fairly but also invests heavily in health-relevant programs of housing, nutrition, health education, and child care, and draws the income floor for everyone higher and more uniformly; in short, it assures the least privileged of its population a higher standard of living. It is likely that the entire package—the interaction of all of these programs—is a major source of Sweden's superior health performance.

One problem in the international comparisons at issue in the Anderson study, which is also characteristic of research on other aspects of the welfare state, is that the rich countries differ in their scale of organization and hence their degree of complexity—that is, in the number of specialized roles and the concomitant heterogeneity of values and beliefs. Thus, it is often said that it is unfair to compare eight million culturally homogeneous Swedes with two hundred million culturally heterogeneous Americans. Size of population can be easily disposed of. Of the nine welfare-state leaders of table 2, three have large populations (West Germany, Italy, France), six have small populations (Austria, Sweden, Belgium, the Netherlands, Czechoslovakia, East Germany). The seven welfare-state laggards are similarly split (USSR, U.S., Japan, versus Canada, Switzerland, Australia, Israel). As for cultural and social heterogeneity, we have already noted in chapter 3 that the welfare effort of heterogeneous Belgium and Holland is similar to that of homogeneous Sweden. Finally, if we again concentrate on one health output, age-specific mortality rates, we have noted Anderson's finding that these rates are better in Sweden than in Minnesota, which are similar in population size and composition.

There is, in fact, no good evidence for the argument that cultural and social heterogeneity such as that of the United States leads either to poor health performance generally or to high infant mortality specifically. A more sophisticated statement of this argument is that once a country gets rich enough, infant mortality and other measures of health performance inevitably improve enough to reduce the influence of the broad economic and social forces of the environment—poverty, illiteracy, ignorance, gross class differences. Family and personal styles—what people do and do not do for themselves—which vary greatly by race, ethnicity, and religion, then become commanding, in health as in other aspects of living. The argument implies that as rich countries become richer, the structural differences that divide them recede and their unique histories and cultures have greater force, and, further, that within each country, variations by descent (based on race, religion, ethnic-linguistic background) will attain dominant influence. It is a version of the thesis that at advanced levels of development the poverty problem becomes increasingly "clinical."

Certainly there are subcultural variations in disease symptoms, definitions of health, and response to agents of the medical system; but the research procedures of those who play up such variations are often misleading. And the issue of the relative importance of poverty versus cultural background in the health and welfare of any substantial population remains unresolved. For instance, Glazer (1971, pp. 74–75) notes "remarkable differences between different ethnic and racial groups in health, even when we hold constant the amount of health care available to these groups. This is easy to illustrate. If we consider Negroes and Puerto Ricans in New York City . . . and we hold constant the socio-economic background of parents, we find startling differences in infant mortality. . . ." "Holding constant" here means comparing the perinatal mortality rates for Negro and Puerto Rican families whose fathers are in the same gross occupational category. At the level of "Professional, Managerial, and Technical" (the most homogeneous category, which itself ranges from physician to draftsman, the manager of Macy's to the manager of a hot-dog stand), the ethnic difference in perinatal mortality is a tiny 1.7 (24.2 for Negroes versus 22.5 for Puerto Ricans). The difference for the most heterogeneous category, "Craftsmen and Operatives" (which itself ranges from thirty-five-year-old high-seniority, high-paid building craftsmen to seventeen-year-old unemployed assembly-line workers) is 8.6 (32.9 for Negroes versus 24.3 for Puerto Ricans), less than the spread of 12.4 *within* Negro strata themselves (36.6 for Negro "Laborers and Service Workers" versus 24.2 for Negro "Professional, Managerial, and Technical"). The gross income data typically gathered in surveys not dealing mainly with income are even worse in quality.[5]

If we were to take the problem of controlling for health-relevant social and economic environment seriously, we would compare the health experiences of such racial and ethnic groups using education of father and mother as an indicator of health information and attitudes, and match the groups by type of housing and neighborhood according to environmental health risks (for instance, whether there are garbage and rats in the alley). And if, in order to sift out the subcultural differences affecting utilization and health, we were to "hold constant the amount of health care available to these groups," we would be forced to gather data on their access to the relevant health care. That assertions about access, let alone the *effect* of access, are so doubtful for only two minority groups in New York City suggests that more ambitious comparisons of the meaning of welfare spending for real welfare in several countries are formidable.

In short, while anything can be defined and measured, if we encounter obstacles in using such solid indicators of welfare output as age-specific mortality rates, we can expect even greater trouble when we tackle such phenomena as the sense of security or anxiety, attachment or alienation, happiness or despair, and try to trace them to particular national policies. Great ingenuity will be required to assess the major effects of the welfare state.

5. On these problems of heterogeneity in "controls" in survey research, see Wilensky, 1966a.

SECTOR SPECIALIZATION:
DOES ONE PROGRAM DRIVE OUT ANOTHER?

The Impact
of the
Welfare State on
Real Welfare

Added to the complexity of gauging both the short-run and long-run effects of welfare effort is the question of sector specialization where one program drives out another. Just as a heavy military burden under modern conditions retards welfare performance, heavy spending on social security may bring neglect of higher education (Austria, Italy). And neglect of social security may be linked to an extremely generous development of higher education (U.S., Israel, USSR, Canada, Australia).

Exploratory data on social security spending by program suggest that despite the general expansion of the whole package, there is a tendency for social security systems to mature in the directions from which they start. If a country early invests a great deal in public health services, it is unlikely to have generous pensions by the measure of earnings replacement rates (U.K. and, if we can trust impressions of observers cutting through the official statute, the USSR). Or if a large fraction of its total social security spending goes to both health services and pensions, its family allowances will appear late and remain meager (Sweden, West Germany). Conversely, if it early specializes in generous family allowances, the fraction of its total spending devoted to pensions will be low (Belgium).

The effect of early sector specialization is apparent in the history of social security in the United States. It first went in for workmen's compensation; the government adopted a job-injury law for federal employees in 1908, and by 1911 ten states had adopted similar laws. Then, in 1935, it moved to old-age and survivors' insurance and unemployment compensation. By the mid-sixties, although by the standards of welfare-state leaders its social security benefits were low, the United States had become a specialist in pensions. It allocated a larger fraction of its total welfare spending to pensions (OASDI) than any of the twenty-two richest countries. Again, this reflects no great public generosity to the aged, whose pensions remain low; it merely underscores the neglect of the rest of the social security package. It is likely that family allowances and national health insurance, if they are adopted at all, will lag in their development.

If we concentrate on benefits per capita, there is some indication of a trade-off between services flowing to the young, such as education, and services devoted to the aged. Consistent with this hypothesis is the pattern of enrollment in higher education in 1966 shown in table 4. Of the seven leaders in mass higher education (U.S. 40, USSR 30, Canada 21, Israel 20, Netherlands 16, Australia 16, Belgium 15), the four for which pension benefit data are available (U.S., Canada, Netherlands, Belgium) are more or less stingy in earnings replacement rates of their old-age pensions (they rank low to middling among the thirteen of our rich countries analyzed in Horlick, 1970).

An accent on youth in some countries is further evident in overlapping payments of (1) family allowances to the parents of children in school or training (up to their middle twenties) and simultaneously (2) educational grants to the same students designed to help them through college. We do not know the incidence and location of these overlapping payments. The cult of youth is supposed to be strictly an American product; the accent on spending for youth to the neglect of the aged, however, may be shared by the USSR, East Germany, Australia, and Israel alike. The point remains speculative. Only more intensive examination of long-term trends in both welfare effort by type of program (proportion of GNP, proportion of total social security spending, proportion of total government spending) and welfare output by type of program (earnings replacement rates of pensions, indicators of physical and mental health, and other measures of benefits and their distribution) will permit a firm judgment of these trade-offs. The necessary data are not yet available.

These trade-offs may slow down the rate of expansion of one program or another. Nevertheless, considering that expenditures for all programs rise and, further, that the biggest spenders among the richest countries do well across the board for all major programs—with the definite exception of higher education and the possible exception of family allowances—we can best view sector specialization as a minor variation on a major theme. The orchestration of the welfare state—the dynamics of its development—moves rich countries toward the interdependence of programs and their integration with general economic policy, including the attack on poverty.

The Impact of the Welfare State on Real Welfare

ASSESSING CRITICISMS OF THE WELFARE STATE

Throughout this book I have emphasized the lack of comparative data for a thorough evaluation of either the conservative and radical attacks on the welfare state or the liberal defense of it. Insofar as my analysis of the convergence and divergence of welfare ideology and practice can help make the complex and elusive target of controversy more concrete, it may make the debate more fruitful. And insofar as it frames new questions and specifies gaps in the evidence, it may encourage research that will permit more informed dialogue.

Does the welfare state work? If the focus is on its effects on the equality of income distribution in some recent year, there are more than hints in English and German data that as a whole the impact is substantially egalitarian. Conservative critics who are repelled by the push for equality should be opposed to this development; radical critics who really want income redistribution should calm down—or at least become aware that their central concern is to "get" the rich, not to improve the economic position of the poor. As for the long run, no one knows how to compare all the transactions between the taxpayers and beneficiaries of 1974 with all the transactions between today's taxpayers and beneficiaries, on the one hand, and their children and grandchildren, on the other. If the focus is not on economic equality but on psychological and economic security, the case for the welfare state seems plain. Does anyone believe that the family or any other overloaded institution could soften the risks of modern life as effectively as the seven or eight major social security programs do?

Does the welfare state reward the idle and improvident, thereby reducing the incentive to work? If every aged person has a decent pension of stable value and none is forced into premature retirement, penalized for his healthy survival and continued eagerness to work; if young people have diversified opportunities for education with generous provisions for loans and subsidies and an employment service linked to the schools that guides them through the maze of early jobs; if the costs and risks of childbearing are reduced and if mothers who want to work are encouraged to do so by provision of good child-care facilities; if everyone can enjoy access to medical facilities at nominal cost; if strenuous efforts are made to eliminate slums; if the risks of unemployment are reduced and the unemployed receive not only compensation but increasingly effective public service in relocating and retraining; if decent living standards are guaranteed for children, widows, invalids, and the handicapped, while efforts are made to provide them with appropriate education and work; if job-injured workers are compensated at levels sufficient to give employers an incentive to improve safety—how will these measures weaken the moral fiber of the nation?

Insofar as there is evidence of the effects of cash welfare benefits on the incentive to work, it shows little, if any, reduced motivation, although there is obviously some very low level of wages and some very high level of welfare payments where a strong temptation to accept the psychological costs of avoiding work could be set up. When the United States government carried out its famous experiments with the negative income tax in New Jersey and Pennsylvania, it paid experimental groups of low-income families various amounts of cash, averaging $100 per month for three years, and paid control groups, matched for original income, nothing. After stratifying the sample by income, the groups were assigned randomly. Controls for race, age, and family composition were applied in the analysis. Although the studies are numerous and the findings complex, they tend to show that none of eight systems of supplementary cash payments had an important effect on the propensity to work among family heads and husband-wife families. Low-income white wives who at the outset were working few hours at very low wages, however, did reduce their work and earnings. And welfare-subsidized young workers took a bit longer to search for jobs, typically ending up in better jobs at higher wages. Other long-term experiments are in progress in Indiana, Colorado, Washington, and rural Iowa and North Carolina (U.S. Department of Health, Education and Welfare, 1973; cf. Watts and Cain, 1973).[6] (The custom of righteously insisting on elaborate evaluation research as a way of avoiding action may not be exclusively American. But one American student of this phenomenon, projecting the rate of increase in expenditure on such poverty experiments in progress and proposed in 1972, concluded that by the 1980s every citizen of the United States could be paid either as a poverty researcher or as a subject in a poverty experiment—a novel way of cleaning up "the welfare mess.")

"Radical" critics, while asserting that the welfare state is inegalitarian—another "rip-off" of the poor by the rich—offer the contradictory claim that social security is successful enough in pacifying the working class (or the poor, or oppressed minorities) that it draws the fangs of the revolutionary tiger. It is indeed possible that the welfare state at its highest level of development reduces the credibility of alienated intellectuals and radical social critics, dampens enthusiasm for mass protest movements, and increases the unemployment rate among revolutionary cadres. That is to say, when a large measure of equality, security, and social justice is achieved, radicals are transformed into reformers, and proletarian unrest is channeled into tame demands for better wages and welfare benefits.

Although the welfare state thus reduces the demand for

6. For earlier discussions of why modern populations remain so work-oriented, see Wilensky, 1961 and 1966b.

blunderbuss attacks on "the system" (the supply of these attacks may remain steady), it increases the need for more sharply focused social criticism. First, by the agencies' own standards, none of these programs is as effective as it might be; and their own standards require continual reexamination in relation to other public purposes. Second, when obvious mass inequities and insecurities are alleviated, less obvious troubles move to the forefront. Just as wages are extremely important to workers who receive relatively meager wages, but not so important to workers who enjoy high wages, so, too, the citizen of a functioning welfare state may respond favorably to social critics who point to worker alienation, inefficient bureaucracies, invasions of privacy and similar abuses of power, private and public—problems that can excite mainly those who already enjoy a decent income and a secure, rising standard of living. That in Sweden a campaign to make subway entrances more accessible to the handicapped could catch on so easily and could force the creation of a commission to consider how to make the entire transportation-communication system better serve the needs of the handicapped is possible partly because major campaigns for larger underprivileged groups were successful in the past. Thus, radical critics are right about co-optation: pensions, health insurance, social assistance, workmen's compensation, and aid to the handicapped may bore them, but these programs, like the rest of the welfare state, greatly interest working-class leaders, minority-group leaders, as well as the great rank and file. If the activists did not find meaningful jobs as professional reformers in and out of the establishment and if the masses of ordinary people did not experience a gain in equality and security, it is conceivable that they would be manning the barricades in a way that would make the most sectarian radicals happy.

Whatever their political persuasion, critics of the welfare state share a tendency to select particular segments of programs, impute utopian goals to them (too often based on the agency's own exaggerated claims) and then conclude that the action falls short. Read the literature on each of these programs and you will find repeated declarations that one or another social policy or program is not the right instrument for dealing with some long-standing social problem. There is first the obvious fact that among the welfare-state laggards, newer, innovative programs are typically funded for such a short period at such a meager level that the fuss about their failure to solve some huge problem is absurd. This was true of most of the programs constituting the "war on poverty" of the early 1960s in the United States; these programs were hardly launched before they were shot down in a cloud of complaints about corruption, costs, welfare scandals. In the rare case where careful evaluations of such programs are made, and evidence is found of some modest success, the results are pronounced as benedictions at the graveside.

Attacks on the more expensive mainstream programs of the welfare state are similarly irrelevant or utopian: A good, expensive education system will not drastically redistribute income; a good, expensive housing program will not drastically reduce crime, delinquency, urban decay; a good, expensive rapid transit system will not immediately stop traffic jams and pollution; a good, expensive health-care system will not greatly improve health; good nutrition and improved sanitation will not overnight reduce nonepidemic disease. But a comparison of educational systems might show that some teach students to read and write critically and coherently and others do not. Similar comparisons of housing programs might show variation in the satisfaction of residents with their housing, and differences in access and cost. The time, cost, and comfort of alternative transportation systems can be compared. And, as we have seen, health-care systems can be assessed cross-nationally; differences in utilization, cost, and the distribution of care can be pinned down; even some effects on health can be inferred.

If in terms of the social indicators listed in this chapter the cost-effectiveness of each major program could be shown by comparison with its alternatives to be wanting, the overriding desire for equal access to a public service would nevertheless

111

stand as a reasonable goal in itself. That the British government at low relative cost can ensure access to physicians for nearly everyone, that the Swedish government can ensure equality of access to an entire range of medical services of somewhat better quality at somewhat greater cost, and that Americans, at the Swedish level of health expenditure, do not provide equitable access, are important measures of national performance. Put another way, sharp differences in access to medical care are significant although the leading causes of death in these countries are the same (heart disease, cancer, and stroke); they would be impressive even if the incidence of disease by social class were identical (which no one yet knows); they would remain important even if several other indicators of health performance were identical. In any case, so few social scientists undertake such studies that intellectual debates about medical services and health research remain almost purely ideological, uncontaminated by reliable, relevant comparisons of countries with contrasting systems.

Finally, critics seldom ask, "What is the cumulative effect of all these interacting programs and their general integration with other socially supportive services?" Just as we cannot judge the redistributive effects of welfare taxing and spending in isolation from one another, so we must consider the interdependence of the economic and social effects of increasingly comprehensive social security schemes. A promising strategy for such study is the intensive comparison of selected welfare-state leaders and laggards outlined in chapter 3.

Students of the welfare state should try to avoid the trap in which mass-media researchers were caught during recent decades—a narrow technicism. What effect did a TV program or a movie have on children? Give the subjects an attitude or skill test before exposure, expose them to the show, then repeat the test. Ergo, the media have little effect: those children already anxious about violence (or whatever) were the ones who suffered; others were insulated by their healthy predispositions, inoculated against harmful TV by a stable family life. This is only a mild caricature of the typical evaluation of media effects. Of course, the critical question is "What is the cumulative effect of sustained media exposure over all the child's years, the interaction of broadcast media and print, of reading, listening, viewing and media talk?" Asking the analogous question about pensions, health insurance, family allowances, social assistance, and education produced hints of the interdependence of most and, sometimes, the cross-purposes of a few (higher education versus the rest).

One group of critics, both radical and conservative, are fond of phrases like "statism," "bureaucratic pathologies," the "arrogance" or "repressiveness" of the government. While comparative welfare administration is beyond the scope of this book, there are many indications that things are not the same everywhere. Can the operation of a new and growing agency with top political priority, like the Office of Economic Opportunity or the National Aeronautics and Space Administration in the sixties in the United States, be the same as that of a routine agency like the United States Office of Education? It is in the latter, not in the former, that one discovers geological layers of doctrine and practice—a vested interest in the fresh ideas of 1922. I have the further impression that, despite a scattering of remarkably imaginative and effective officials and staff experts in every country, the higher and middle civil services tend to be overblown and cautious in Austria; expert but variably isolated in France; inefficient and octogenarian in Italy; incorruptible and young in Sweden; traditional, hidebound, yet professional and dedicated in West Germany and Britain. If such impressions reflect reality, then surely the relation of citizens to officials must vary in these countries. The Scandinavian ombudsmen, independently policing the bureaucracy, must inhibit some excesses.

Finally, it is not at all obvious that the arrogance of a welfare bureaucrat in control of an employment agency necessarily exceeds the arrogance of a private industrial executive in control of an oil supply. Or if the issue is interpersonal contact between service personnel and clients, can the officiousness of the medical receptionist in a large public hospital exceed the officiousness of a private secretary who controls access to her boss with exquisite sensitivity to social status?

It is said that public bureaucracies are by nature self-expanding, self-aggrandizing, and thus impossible to phase out when they have outlived their usefulness. That is supposedly one of the great risks of trying to choke a problem with money—what pours into the administrative apparatus does not typically come out in benefits and services.

This iron law of Parkinson is like the iron law of Michels. Although it provides general orientation it obscures all the interesting variations within which people act out their daily lives. Plainly, it is easier to cut back budgets of agencies than to reduce personnel; and clearly it is not easy to eliminate both completely. There is some comparative evidence from social security systems that in the late 1960s administrative costs were climbing faster than benefits (Fisher, 1971, p. 11). But the problem was concentrated among the less developed countries; modernization does appear to make bureaucracies a bit more efficient.

Efficiency aside, obsolete programs or parts of programs are often bent to new and even creative purposes. Family allowances in France may be frivolous and ineffective in their original purpose of increasing fertility, although they have surely been effective in producing a pronatalist clientele well organized to lobby for expanded benefits. But family allowances do lend themselves to reverse incentives with a modified schedule of payments (that is, childless couples can be rewarded, families of five disqualified). More important than their use or misuse in population policy, family allowances, as we have seen, can serve as the back-door entry for an otherwise unpalatable antipoverty program. For those who favor a socially adequate income as a matter of right, such a result is not bad. A more direct and efficient way to accomplish that task is some form of negative income tax,[7] but if, after long educational and propaganda efforts, these schemes everywhere arouse such passionate opposition that they are doomed to defeat, then such feasible means as family allowances—almost universally acceptable—are preferable.

The oldest conservative criticism of the rise of the welfare state has its roots deep in the tradition of classical economics. It asserts the interdependence of economic individualism and civil liberties. Without lively free markets in goods, services, and labor, democratic liberties cannot flourish. If everyone becomes a dependent client of the bureaucratic state, the virtues of self-reliance, as well as the independence of mind and spirit, erode, inevitably giving way to an oppressive collectivism.

Perhaps at some high level of government spending, under some additional conditions undermining the structural and normative supports for civil liberties, the welfare state might be a threat to democracy. But nothing in the history of welfare-state development among the twenty-two countries covered in this book suggests such a relationship. In the absence of systematic studies of trends in civil liberties among welfare-state leaders and laggards, we will have to rely on common knowledge. Since World War II, civil liberties have surely not been threatened as much in the Netherlands and Sweden, countries at the top of any measure of welfare spending and output, as they have suffered in the United States, Canada, and Japan, three of our welfare-state laggards. Indeed, the great tolerance and libertarian traditions of the Dutch have retained their vitality since the sixteenth century. And neither the Dutch nor the Swedes appear to lack either discipline or independence of spirit.

This is not to deny that an enraged middle class, threatened

7. These plans guarantee a certain payment if the household receives no other income and reduce this payment by a certain percentage (the tax rate) of every dollar the household earns up to some breakeven level at which the payment is reduced to zero.

by "stagflation," might in the future rebel against the egalitarian drift of modern society and find among its scapegoats both the poorer beneficiaries of the welfare state and the intellectuals who claim to articulate the discontents of the oppressed. Although such a development could be more a product of events in international relations, monetary systems, and trade balances, and of energy and food shortages than resistance to the welfare state, it is a threat we must not ignore.

WELFARE STATE VERSUS WELFARE SOCIETY

In the United States in the mid-sixties and early seventies, the revolt of the middle mass was expressed in the election of California's Governor Ronald Reagan (1966 and 1970) and President Richard Nixon (1968 and 1972); at the same time it drove Mayor John Lindsay out of office in New York City.

This growing middle mass consists of the upper working class—a mass of craftsmen in the building, printing, and other trades, foremen, and high-paid operatives, on the one hand; and the lower middle class—a mass of clerks, salesmen, small entrepreneurs, managers with few subordinates, semiprofessional, semitechnical people, on the other. As I have argued elsewhere (1960, 1961, 1965), the lines between these two strata are blurring in the precise sense that their behavior and values are closer to one another than to the adjacent occupational and income strata above and below. I believe that as rich countries become richer, the middle mass as a political force becomes more fluid, torn loose from traditional political identities; and more strategic, larger and more potent as a swing vote. While most apparent in the United States, this tendency, as I have suggested in chapters 2 and 3, is no American monopoly.

Looking up, the citizen of the American middle mass sees the overprivileged, college-educated upper middle class and the rich, who seem to evade taxes, live well, let their children run wild at expensive colleges—or worse, at state universities, at his expense. Moreover, the overprivileged seem often to be in alliance with the poor, with the blacks from whom he has escaped to a middle-mass suburb, with welfare mothers whose morals and skin color repel him, with the countercultural young lazing about in college or on welfare or, worse, demonstrating in the street. While such repulsive people complain about the "sick society," the citizen of the middle mass works hard at a disciplined job, struggles for a decent safe house, higher wages and more safety and freedom on the job, better, more narrowly "vocational" schools for his children, and, of course, a full range of consumer "goodies"—cars and campers, home appliances such as washing machines, dryers, garbage disposals, dishwashers, as well as color TV, and perhaps wall-to-wall carpeting.

In short, he sees an unholy alliance of the immoral poor, despised minorities, lazy, undisciplined, unpatriotic youth and their friends among the libertarian educated. When the coalition tells him that the poverty he happily escaped must be wiped out at his expense and that racial minorities must take over his job, his neighborhood, his children's school, he is understandably indignant.

The welfare state, as I suggested in chapter 2, can be made to symbolize his grievances; his discontents can be channeled into a tough, repressive law-and-order coalition directed against both the liberal segments of the educated classes and the poor. The welfare state, he vaguely perceives, is not so much for him as for people with a privileged education and for the nonworking poor.

Among welfare-state leaders the revolt of the middle mass has been limited partly because political elites committed to the welfare state have mobilized a strongly organized working class that reaches down to the poor and up to lower-white-collar strata, and partly because the benefits are substantial and widespread. Nevertheless, as welfare, health, and education costs soar and the tax burdens of the middle mass grow heavier, the potential for welfare backlash greatly increases (see chapter 3).

To keep educated strata in coalition with major segments of the labor movement and the middle mass is increasingly difficult. The educated are concerned with challenging work for themselves, high-quality education for their children, and the protection of their privileges and status; their political consciousness is increasingly bent toward ecological, aesthetic, and similar issues symbolized in the slogan "quality of life." They begin to believe that social-democratic governments are preoccupied with the older problems of an industrial society—a society which in the new mythology of the educated is no longer there, having become "post-industrial."

If a humane welfare state is to be further advanced in combination with traditional democratic liberties, the developing political rage of the middle mass must be dampened and the educated—radicals, liberals, and conservatives alike—must come to respect the ordinary desires of ordinary people. This implies the creation of new political coalitions which can connect hard economic issues—the redistributional issues of the welfare state, the issues of employment and inflation—that preoccupy the middle mass with the issues of environmental degradation, consumer protection, and foreign policy that preoccupy the affluent (Wilensky, 1972). In short, the problem is to humanize the welfare state and make it more effective at a time when costs are climbing, and simultaneously to transform it into a welfare society that can cope with universal issues of civilized survival.

It is a melancholy possibility that the welfare state at its most advanced level diverts political energy, expert talent, and economic resources away from the newly publicized problems of pollution and population control, urban decay and resource exhaustion. Neither political elites nor informed publics among the welfare-state leaders demonstrate deep concern about the degradation of the environment; nor have they developed an ecology movement comparable to that of the United States, a welfare laggard; nor can they match the more elitist and more powerful environmental and conservation lobbies of Britain, a middle-rank welfare spender. The French government stands paralyzed before the pollution of Paris; the Italians cannot cope

with the destruction of Venice or the traffic in Rome. After
World War II, Germany, blessed with defeat, moved swiftly not
only to perfect a benign welfare state, not only to conquer world
markets, but also to help the French make the Rhine one of the
dirtiest rivers in the world.

The welfare state is in the process of humanizing industrial
society. Over a century it has meant great gains in economic and
psychological security for the least privileged; in the short run of
each generation it produces some income redistribution. It is a
prime source of consensus and social order in modern society,
pluralist or totalitarian.

It would be ironic, therefore, if the welfare state should
prevent the emergence of the welfare society. For if the
guarantees of minimum standards of income, nutrition, health,
housing, and education are to be effective, they must now be
matched by guarantees of breathable air, potable water, and
safety from sudden violence and slow poison—or they become
rights without meaning.

Appendix on Methods

Countries were included in the cross-sectional analysis for the year 1966 if data were available for all of the following: (1) GNP at factor cost in national currency units and in U.S. dollars; and per capita GNP at factor cost in U.S. dollars; (2) social security spending; and (3) military spending. All the countries of the world for which these data are available are included in table 4.

For time-series analysis we selected 22 "rich" nations. From a list of 114 independent polities having populations of one million or more in 1966, ranked by the *World Bank Atlas* on per capita GNP at factor cost, in U.S. dollars, in that year, we chose the upper one-fifth (23 nations) for which data are available on GNP, military spending (all or most years between 1950 and 1970) and social security spending (selected years 1949–1966). Of this list of 23, Venezuela, the lowest in per capita GNP, was dropped because it was suspected that as an "enclave economy" it was not comparable to the other 22 countries for purposes of our analysis.

There is a slight discrepancy between the sample selected for time-series analysis and the richest 22 countries of the cross-sectional analysis: while Hungary ranks slightly above

TABLE 4: *Social Security and Military Spending as a Percent of GNP at Factor Cost and Enrollment Ratios for Total Population 20–24 in Higher Education in 1965 or Nearest Year for 64 Countries Ranked by Per Capita GNP at Factor Cost, 1966*

Country[a] (ranked by per capita GNP for 1966)	Per capita GNP[b] in U.S. dollars (1966)	Social security spending[c] as percent of GNP (1966)	Military spending[d] as percent of GNP (1966)	Enrollment ratios for total population 20–24 in higher education, 1965 or nearest year[e]
United States	3,542	7.9	9.1	40
Sweden	2,677	17.5	4.4	12
Iceland	2,551	8.7	0.0	6
Switzerland	2,335	9.5	2.8	6
Canada	2,288	10.1	3.6	21
Denmark	1,997	13.9	3.1	13
Australia	1,980	9.0	3.8	16
New Zealand	1,940	11.8	2.2	14
Luxembourg	1,926	17.5	1.6	3
Germany (FR)	1,871	19.6	4.7	9
France	1,866	18.3	5.9	14
Norway	1,819	12.6	4.0	8
Belgium	1,690	18.5	3.3	15
Finland	1,657	13.1	1.8	11
United Kingdom	1,532	14.4	6.5	10
Netherlands	1,497	18.3	4.1	16
Czechoslovakia	1,334	17.2	6.3	14
Israel	1,275	8.3	11.9	20
Germany (East)	1,227	16.4	4.5	13
Austria	1,225	21.0	1.5	9
USSR	1,181	10.1	12.2	30
Italy	1,097	17.5	3.8	12
Japan	952	6.2	1.0	12
Hungary	895	8.8	3.5	7
Ireland	882	11.1	1.5	12

TABLE 4 (*continued*)   *Appendix*

Country[a] (ranked by per capita GNP for 1966)	Per capita GNP[b] in U.S. dollars (1966)	Social security spending[c] as percent of GNP (1966)	Military spending[d] as percent of GNP (1966)	Enrollment ratios for total population 20–24 in higher education, 1965 or nearest year[e]
Venezuela	820	3.8	2.4	6
Poland	762	9.3	5.7	13
Bulgaria	721	10.5	4.0	17
Trinidad-Tobago	721	3.4	0.7	2
Spain	713	4.3	3.3	6
Rumania	705	8.0	2.8	10
Greece	660	12.0	4.2	10
Cyprus	652	2.3	2.0	1
Panama	501	6.7	0.2	7
Mexico	493	2.9	0.8	4
Jamaica	469	3.0	0.6	1
Uruguay	442	8.3	1.8	9
Yugoslavia	424	11.6	4.9	13
Portugal	404	5.8	6.0	5
Costa Rica	336	2.9	0.6	6
Nicaragua	318	2.9	1.6	2
Colombia	285	1.3	1.4	3
Guyana	281	4.9	0.5	1
Guatemala	279	2.2	1.2	2
Malaysia	272	3.5	5.4	2
Iraq	270	1.2	11.4	4
Turkey	269	2.0	5.2	4
El Salvador	254	2.6	1.3	2
Ghana	239	1.4	2.3	1
Honduras	221	1.1	1.4	1
Zambia	215	3.8	2.4	..
China (Taiwan)	214	1.4	12.8	..
Ecuador	212	3.2	2.5	4

Country[a] (ranked by per capita GNP for 1966)	Per capita GNP[b] in U.S. dollars (1966)	Social security spending[c] as percent of GNP (1966)	Military spending[d] as percent of GNP (1966)	Enrollment ratios for total population 20–24 in higher education, 1965 or nearest year[e]
Paraguay	206	2.2	3.2	3
Brazil	192	8.2	3.8	2
Syria	176	1.0	10.2	8
Tunisia	168	4.4	2.2	2
Ceylon	139	3.9	0.9	2
Togo	115	2.2	1.6	1
Cameroon	110	1.8	2.7	1
Pakistan	104	0.6	4.0	3
India	67	1.4	4.9	3
Burma	62	1.1	7.2	1
Upper Volta	50	2.8	1.2	1

[a] All countries for which data on social security spending, military spending, and GNP at factor cost were available for 1966.

[b] Factor cost GNP is used instead of market price GNP to make more valid comparisons of countries that vary in their reliance on indirect taxes. See Appendix on Methods.

[c] The source for social security expenditures for all countries except East Germany was the ILO, *The Cost of Social Security, 1964–66* (Geneva: 1972), pp. 317–323. East German data are from the Bundesministerium für innerdeutsche Beziehungen, *Bericht des Bundesregierung und Materialien zur Lage der Nation, 1971* (Bonn: 1971), p. 397.

[d] The source for military expenditures for all countries except the USSR, Australia, and New Zealand was the U.S. Arms Control and Disarmament Agency, *World Military Expenditures, 1971* (Washington: 1972), pp. 18–21. For the USSR see the Institute for Strategic Studies, *The Military Balance, 1972–1973* (London: 1973), p. 73. For Australia and New Zealand see the Stockholm International Peace Research Institute, *SIPRI Yearbook of World Armaments and Disarmaments, 1969–70* (Uppsala: 1970), pp. 274–276.

[e] Total number enrolled divided by total number age 20–24. UNESCO, *Statistical Yearbook, 1971* (Louvain, Belgium: UNESCO, 1972), table 2.7, pp. 101–119.

Ireland on per capita GNP at factor cost in table 4, Ireland but
not Hungary is included in the sample of 22. This is due to the
relative weakness of the estimate of Hungary's GNP (see p. 132).

SOCIAL SECURITY EXPENDITURE DATA

The main source of data on social security expenditures for the
period 1949–1966 is the International Labour Office, *The Cost
of Social Security: Seventh International Inquiry, 1964–1966*
(Geneva, 1972, pp. 317–323). The figure used was "total
expenditure" on social security in national currency units at
current prices for the years reported. The criteria adopted by the
ILO for the definition of "social security" follow: "(1) the
objective of the system must be to grant curative or preventive
medical care, or to maintain income in case of involuntary loss
of earnings or of an important part of earnings, or to grant
supplementary incomes to persons having family responsibilities;
(2) the system must have been set up by legislation which
attributes specific individual rights to, or which imposes specified obligations on, a public, semi-public or autonomous body;
(3) the system should be administered by a public, semi-public
or autonomous body. . . . However, any scheme of employ-
ment-injury compensation should be included in the inquiry,
even if it does not meet the criterion in (3) above, because the
compensation of employment injuries is imposed directly on
the employer" (*The Cost of Social Security*, 1972, p. 2). Thus,
the ILO includes "compulsory social insurance, certain voluntary social insurance schemes, family allowance schemes, special
schemes for public employees, public health services, public
assistance, and benefits granted to war victims." In all cases
important welfare and health programs which have been insti-
tuted by legislation are included in the expenditure figures used
in the tables (e.g., the National Health Service in the United
Kingdom, national health insurance schemes in other countries).
Certain nonstatutory voluntary schemes are excluded: "voluntary or optional insurance not covered by criteria (2) and (3)

above, and legal or contractual obligations under which the employer is required to pay benefits directly in respect of contingencies other than employment injury" (ibid., p. 2). The least comparable category included in ILO's aggregate figure is "public assistance" or "social assistance," but that tends to be so small relative to the major programs that it poses no problem for the purposes of analysis in this book.

Social security expenditure data for the Common Market countries (except Luxembourg, which is excluded from the time-series analysis) for the years 1967 through 1970 are taken from the Office Statistique des Communautés Européennes, *Les comptes sociaux dans la Communauté européenne,* 1962–1970 (Luxembourg, 1972). The European Communities' definition of social expenditure (*dépense sociale*) is somewhat broader than the ILO definition of "social security." The EC's *dépense sociale* includes the following public expenditures covering individual and household risks and needs (see the *annexe méthologique* of the *Comtes Sociaux* publication, p. 87):

DÉPENSE SOCIALE	Toute dépense entraînée par la couverture des charges résultant pour les ménages, de l'apparition ou de l'existence de certains risques ou besoins, dans la mesure où cette dépense donne lieu à l'intervention d'un "tiers", c'est-à-dire d'une unité autre que les ménages eux-mêmes—administration ou entreprise (publiques ou privées)—et sans pour autant qu'il y ait simultanément contrepartie équivalente du bénéficiare.
LISTE PROVISOIRE	—maladie
DES RISQUES OU	—vieillesse, décè, survie
BESOINS	—invalidité —infirmité physique ou psychique —accident du travail, maladie professionnelle —chômage —charges de famille —événement politique et calamité naturelle

To call attention to the definitional differences, the vertical line in table 2 (p. 30) separates the pre-1967 ILO data from the EC data for 1967–1970. Although the EC definition is broader and its estimates therefore higher, differences between figures from the two sources are quite small. Expressed in absolute percentage differences between ratios of social security spending to GNP using the two sources—the EC ratio minus the ILO ratio—the average differences over the period 1964–1965 are as follows: 0.5 for Belgium; 2.8 for France; 1.9 for West Germany; 2.9 for Italy; and 1.8 for the Netherlands. Comparing rank orders of these five nations on social security spending as a percent of GNP for 1966, a substitution of the EC figure for the ILO results in no change for West Germany, and only very small changes (one rank or less) for France, Italy, and the Netherlands. Belgium, however, drops from second to fifth; but the difference in percent between the first and fifth ranks in the EC series is only 2.8 and in the ILO series only 2.1.

The ILO does not report data for East Germany. We relied on the West German Bundesministerium für innerdeutsche Beziehungen, *Bericht des Bundesregierung und Materialien zur Lage der Nation,* 1971 (Bonn, 1971, p. 397), which attempts to match East and West categories. This publication lists "total net expenditures" for "social welfare" for both East and West Germany, 1965–1968. In order to ascertain whether the concept of "social security" used in compiling the expenditure data for this volume was comparable to that of the ILO, the figures for West Germany from the two sources were compared for the two years where they overlap. Differences in the two sources for West Germany for 1965 and 1966 are miniscule. For 1965, the ratio of social security spending to GNP at factor cost using ILO data was 19.0 percent; using Bundesministerium data for the same year, this ratio was 19.4 percent. For 1966, the results are nearly as good (19.6 percent versus 20.1 percent). On the basis of these very small differences between the two sources for West Germany, we can infer with reasonable confidence that the East

German estimate is implicitly based on a concept of "social security" equivalent to that of the ILO.

However, there still remains the problem of comparability of such data across nations, especially when some of the nations are "communist" and some "capitalist." In order to assess the validity of the ILO data for "communist" nations, we have compared our figures for social security spending with those of Frederic Pryor (1968). Pryor makes an heroic attempt to construct comparable time-series of health and welfare expenditures for fourteen communist and capitalist nations. His careful, original estimates of social security spending (i.e., health plus welfare) were made independently of the ILO, and thus constitute a check on our use of the ILO figures. Again, the results of such a comparison are heartening. The average absolute percentage differences between Pryor's data and the ILO's for the years they both report are small: Austria, +0.6; Czechoslovakia, +2.5; Ireland, +2.4; Italy, +0.5; USSR, +0.7; United States, +0.2; and West Germany, −0.6.[1]

In short, the ILO data on social security spending for the rich "communist" countries (USSR and Czechoslovakia) appear to be as reliable as those for the "capitalist" countries; the East German estimates produced by West German sources are comparable; and in general, the measures from diverse sources are surprisingly interchangeable.

MILITARY EXPENDITURE DATA

The sources tapped for military expenditure data in all tables are the U.S. Arms Control and Disarmament Agency, *World*

1. These differences are in percent of GNP at factor cost devoted to social security. The figure is derived by subtracting the ILO ratio of social security to GNP (expressed in percent) from the Pryor ratio of "health plus welfare" to GNP (the same denominator) for each year the two sources report data on the same country. For all countries except the Soviet Union, these overlapping years are 1952, 1955, 1958, and 1961; for the USSR no data are available from the ILO for 1952. The differences for each country over these years were summed and divided by the number of observations to arrive at an "average difference."

Military Expenditures, 1971 (ACDA); the Institute for Strategic Studies (London), *The Military Balance* (ISS); and the Stockholm International Peace Research Institute, *SIPRI Yearbook of World Armaments and Disarmaments, 1969–70* (SIPRI). The time-series for military spending was constructed from figures reported in all three sources. The exact source cited for each country for each year is found in the notes to the table; the reasons for selecting particular sources are explained here. First, for many countries there was only one source which reported military spending data for the period 1950–1960 (viz., SIPRI); here we used the available source. Second, for those countries for which sources overlapped in coverage, we compared sources to uncover possible trouble spots. In all but three cases (USSR, New Zealand, and Australia) different sources were consistent. For Australia and New Zealand the figures finally used were SIPRI's; these provide the most complete time-series and are consistent with figures reprinted by ISS for overlapping years. For the Soviet Union, the ISS time-series from *The Military Balance 1972–73* was used.

Inclusions and Exclusions for Military Spending. ACDA defines military expenditures as "current and capital expenditures to meet the needs of the armed forces as follows: expenditures of national defence agencies for military programs; expenditures for the military components of such mixed activities as atomic energy, space, and research and development; military assistance to foreign countries; military stockpiling; retirement pensions for career personnel; and expenditures on certain paramilitary forces" (*World Military Expenditures*, 1971, p. 52). However, it is also noted that "expenditures for veterans' benefits, civil defense, civilian space, strategic industrial stockpiling, and public debt service are excluded" (ibid., p. 55).

SIPRI defines military expenditures to include "the amount of work actually done . . . for military purposes. . . . It is the actual use of resources which we are attempting to measure. . . .

Expenditure is defined to include research and development, to include military aid in the budget of the donor country and to exclude it from the budget of the recipient country, and to exclude war pensions" (*SIPRI Yearbook*, 1969–70, p. 259). In addition, the following caveat is included: "For many countries, however, it was not possible to get a precise definition of the coverage of the figures, and no adjustments were made" (ibid., p. 260).

ISS notes in its most recent edition of *The Military Balance* (1973) that "the figures quoted for defence expenditure are the latest available," but adds that in a comparison with data published previously "the figures will not necessarily correspond" (p. iv)—mainly because of retrospective updating. Despite their limited reporting of time-series, and their cryptic definitions, the ISS is considered by experts to be the most reliable agency monitoring military spending, largely because they use informed judgments to modify official figures; we have used their figures to resolve discrepancies among sources for the USSR, New Zealand, and Australia.

The Soviet Union as a Special Problem. The ISS time-series is the best and most complete available. Nevertheless, there are several formidable problems in making estimates of Soviet military spending. First, the ISS bases its estimate on the official Soviet defense budget. These official figures are then adjusted to *include* military spending concealed in nonmilitary budgetary categories (ISS counts 75 percent of the Soviet science budget as work done for the military), and *exclude* certain types of stockpiling and paramilitary functions such as border guards and civil defense. These adjustments are necessarily approximate. Second, the ISS estimates are expressed in U.S. dollars, which ISS calculates by using a special "defence ruble" exchange rate of 0.40 to 0.50 rubles per dollar. This rate, intended as a purchasing-power equivalent, reflects the relative cheapness of military goods and manpower compared with other Soviet output. Since our dollar GNP figure was explicitly *not* a

purchasing-power equivalent, we converted back to rubles by
dividing the ISS dollar figures by 0.45, and formed the fraction
(Military Spending/GNP) using the *ruble* series of GNP at
adjusted factor cost. The result corresponds quite closely to
Becker's (1969, pp. 163–165). From the point of view of an
expert in Soviet national accounts, using his knowledge of the
Soviet economy, Becker independently estimates a range of
total military spending; he suggests that it must have been
between 7 and 10 percent of GNP at adjusted factor cost in the
years 1958–1964. Our point estimates range from 7.7 percent to
9.8 percent for the same years. A third problem is that strategic
concealment of military spending implies hiding different
amounts in different places in different years, so all the above
estimates for any particular year might be in error by as much as
2 or 3 percentage points. Nevertheless, we are confident that the
figures in table 3 reflect the major trends in Soviet military
spending over this twenty-year period.

GROSS NATIONAL PRODUCT AT FACTOR COST

This measure, rather than the more familiar GNP at market
prices, was used as the denominator of the ratios of social
security spending and military spending to GNP in all tables in
order to obtain a measure unbiased by the differing weights of
indirect taxes in the tax systems of the countries studied and to
make East-West comparisons more valid. The OECD *National
Accounts Statistics of Member Countries* (1968–1970) reports
GNP at factor cost for almost all member countries in almost all
the years 1950–1970. For market-economy countries not reported therein we calculated GNP at factor cost from figures
given in the UN *Yearbook of National Account Statistics*
(various years). Exchange rates were selected after consulting the
International Monetary Fund's *Annual Report on Exchange
Restrictions* (various years) for cases where the official exchange
rates were suspect. Figures for the USSR come from Nancy
Nimitz, *Soviet National Income and Product, 1956–1958*

(which actually presents figures for 1949 to 1958); Abraham Becker, *Soviet National Income 1958–1964*; and three Joint Economic Committee/U.S. Congress compendia: *New Directions in the Soviet Economy* (1966), *Economic Performance and the Military Burden in the Soviet Union* (1970), and *Soviet Economic Prospects for the Seventies* (1973). The extensive recalculation involved in adjusting Soviet figures to the Western concepts of national income and allowing for the divergence between established prices and resource costs render these estimates less reliable than those of market economies. When possible, we have used both direct-dollar estimates and adjusted factor-cost-ruble estimates, rather than attempting conversions by an unrealistic "exchange rate." To make these direct-dollar estimates more comparable with dollar estimates for market economies derived using exchange rates, we reduced them by the average ratio of exchange-rate to purchasing-power-parity GNP among European market economies, as suggested by Hagen and Hawrylyshyn (1969, p. 26).

The same procedure has been followed for other East European countries, though since they have been studied less intensively than the USSR, year-by-year figures could not be presented with the same degree of confidence. We drew dollar values and index numbers from Thad Alton, "Economic Structure and Growth in Eastern Europe," in Joint Economic Committee/U.S. Congress, *Economic Developments in Countries of Eastern Europe* (1970); local-currency values were derived for the base year 1962 from Pryor's figures on spending in national currencies on selected programs and on spending as a fraction of GNP, then they were extrapolated backwards and forwards using the index numbers constructed by Alton. Obviously, these are our least secure estimates; it is for this reason that we have omitted Hungary from the sample chosen for intensive study, although it appears to rank marginally above Ireland in per capita GNP. We are confident that Czechoslovakia, East Germany, and the Soviet Union belong in the "rich" twenty-two by any reasonable estimation.

Enrollment ratios are more reliable than educational expenditure estimates. Although comparing national educational effort measured by enrollment ratios and national welfare effort measured by expenditures is like comparing apples and oranges, this procedure is better than comparing tolerably good apples (data on social security expenditures) and rotten apples (data on educational expenditures).

The enrollment ratios used in these tables have been drawn from the UNESCO *Statistical Yearbook, 1971* (Louvain, Belgium, UNESCO, 1971). The aim of the *Yearbook* is to present figures for the latest year for which data are available, that is, 1968 or 1969. In addition, figures for earlier years have been included for the years nearest to 1960 and 1965. By using these figures a meaningful time-series can be developed. The data presented in the *Yearbook, 1971* differ from corresponding data for the same year given in earlier editions because of revisions based on new information.

Enrollment ratios are simply the number of students enrolled in schools divided by the number of persons in a particular age group. The total higher education enrollment ratios were obtained by dividing the total number of students enrolled in higher education institutions by the number of persons aged 20–24 in the population of the country. The result is expressed in percentages. Female higher-education enrollment ratios were obtained by dividing the number of females in higher education by the number of females aged 20–24 in the population.

Higher education is defined as all institutions at the postsecondary-school level, both degree-granting and non-degree-granting universities, teachers' training colleges, technical colleges, et cetera, both public and private. As far as possible the enrollment figures include part-time students, but those following correspondence courses are generally excluded. Data on enrollment refer solely to students who are eligible to sit exams and receive degrees, diplomas, and certificates.

No female enrollment ratios are reported because they correlate .97 with the total enrollment ratios. If a country provides a large fraction of youth with a chance at post-secondary education, women are swept up along with men, whatever special sorting occurs among curricula and ultimate occupational fate.

TABLE 5: *Simple Correlates of Social Security Spending: 60 Countries*

	(2)	(3)	(4)	(5)	(6)	(7)	(8)	(9)
(1) Age of Social Security System ($\log_e$)	84	61	07	35	−41	−37	32	85
(2) Persons 65 and Over as a Percent of Total Population		74	11	43	−51	−22	20	89
(3) Per Capita GNP at Factor Cost			13	55	−45	−25	−02	67
(4) Military Spending as Percent of GNP at Factor Cost				−14	−10	10	25	08
(5) Liberal Democratic State					−60	−34	−41	45
(6) Oligarchical Authoritarian State						−19	−23	−47
(7) Populist Authoritarian State							−13	−33
(8) Totalitarian State								23
(9) Social Security Spending as Percent of GNP at Factor Cost								

NOTE: Decimal points have been omitted for clarity. Underlined r's are $p < .05$. The list of countries is on pp. 122–124.

TABLE 6: *Simple Correlates of Social Security Spending: 14 Countries*

	(2)	(3)	(4)	(5)	(6)	(7)
(1) Age of Social Security System ($\log_e$)	<u>88</u>	−23	48	03	11	<u>93</u>
(2) Persons 65 and Over as a Percent of Total Population		−32	<u>59</u>	00	14	<u>87</u>
(3) Index of Belief in Planning for Equality			−33	22	−22	−22
(4) Per Capita GNP at Factor Cost				27	24	51
(5) Military Spending as Percent of GNP at Factor Cost					−08	02
(6) Belief in Equality of Opportunity						14
(7) Social Security Spending as a Percent of GNP at Factor Cost						

NOTE: Decimal points have been omitted for clarity. Underlined r's are $p < .05$. The list of countries is on pp. 122–124.

TABLE 7: *Simple Correlates of Social Security Spending: 22 Countries*

	(2)	(3)	(4)	(5)	(6)
(1) Age of Social Security System ($\log_e$)	91	03	54	−04	91
(2) Persons 65 and Over as a Percent of Total Population		−01	62	−09	91
(3) Index of Belief in Planning for Equality			−15	22	01
(4) Per Capita GNP at Factor Cost				23	57
(5) Military Spending as Percent of GNP at Factor Cost					−09
(6) Social Security Spending as a Percent of GNP at Factor Cost					

NOTE: Decimal points have been omitted for clarity. Underlined r's are $p < .05$. The list of countries is on pp. 122–124.

TABLE 8: *Classification of Political Systems by Type: 64 Countries*

Liberal Democratic States	Totalitarian States	Authoritarian Oligarchic States	Authoritarian Populist States
United States	Czechoslovakia	Venezuela	Cyprus
Sweden	Germany (East)	Spain	Mexico
Iceland	USSR	Panama	Guatemala
Switzerland	Hungary	Portugal	Iraq
Canada	Poland	Nicaragua	*Zambia
Denmark	Bulgaria	Colombia	Syria
Australia	Rumania	Malaysia	Tunisia
New Zealand	Yugoslavia	El Salvador	*Cameroon
Luxembourg		Ghana	
Germany (FR)		Honduras	
France		Taiwan	
Norway		Paraguay	
Belgium		Brazil	
Finland		Togo	
United Kingdom		*Pakistan	
Netherlands		*Burma	
Israel		Upper Volta	
Austria			
Italy			
Japan			
Ireland			
Trinidad-Tobago			
Greece (pre-junta)			
Jamaica			
Uruguay			
Costa Rica			
Guyana			
Turkey			
Ecuador			
Ceylon			
India			

NOTE: In each category countries are ranked high to low by per capita GNP for 1966. Countries marked with an asterisk were dropped from the regression analysis because of missing data on the proportion of persons 65 and older in the population.

Bibliography

Aaron, Henry J. 1967. "Social Security: International Comparisons." In *Studies in the Economics of Income Maintenance*, edited by Otto Eckstein. Washington, D.C.: Brookings Institution.

———. 1968. [See Pechman, Aaron, and Taussig, 1968.]

———. 1972. *Shelter and Subsidies: Who Benefits from Federal Housing Policies*. Washington, D.C.: Brookings Institution.

———. 1973. *Why Is Welfare So Hard to Reform?* Washington, D.C.: Brookings Institution.

Abel-Smith, Brian. 1967. *An International Study of Health Expenditure*. Geneva: World Health Organization (WHO Public Health Paper No. 32).

Alton, Thad P. 1970. "Economic Structures and Growth in Eastern Europe." In *Economic Developments in Countries of Eastern Europe*. Joint Economic Committee, Congress of the United States. Washington, D.C.: Government Printing Office.

Ander, O. Fritiof. 1958. *The Building of Modern Sweden; the Reign of Gustav V, 1907–1950*. Rock Island, Illinois: Augustana Book Concern.

Anderson, Odin W. 1972. *Health Care: Can There Be Equity?—The United States, Sweden, and England*. New York: Wiley.

Andreski, Stanislav. 1968. *Military Organization and Society*. 2d enl. ed. Berkeley and Los Angeles: University of California Press.

Ball, Robert. 1973. "How Europe Created Its 'Minority' Problem." *Fortune* 88 (December): 132–142.

Baran, Paul, and Paul Sweezy. 1966. *Monopoly Capital*. New York: Monthly Review Press.

Becker, Abraham S. 1969. *Soviet National Income, 1958–64.* Berkeley and Los Angeles: University of California Press.

Blondel, Jean. 1969. *An Introduction to Comparative Government.* New York: Praeger.

Briggs, Asa. 1961. "The Welfare State in Historical Perspective." *Archives of European Sociology* 11: 221–258.

Bronfenbrenner, Martin. 1971. *Income Distribution Theory.* Chicago: Aldine-Atherton.

Burn, Barbara B. 1971. *Higher Education in Nine Countries.* New York: McGraw-Hill.

Castles, Stephen, and Godula Kosack. 1973. *Immigrant Workers and Class Structure in Western Europe.* London: Oxford University Press.

Conference on Policies for Educational Growth. 1971. *Group Disparities in Educational Participation and Achievement.* Vol. IV. Paris: Organization for Economic Cooperation and Development.

Cutright, Phillips. 1965. "Political Structure, Economic Development, and National Social Security Programs." *American Journal of Sociology* 70: 537–550.

Denison, Edward S. 1967. *Why Growth Rates Differ: Postwar Experience in Nine Western Countries.* Washington, D.C.: Brookings Institution.

Duncan, Otis D. 1966. "Path Analysis: Sociological Examples." *American Journal of Sociology* 72 (July): 1–16.

————. 1969. *Toward Social Reporting: Next Steps.* New York: Russell Sage Foundation.

Durkheim, Emile. 1956. *Education and Sociology.* Glencoe, Illinois: Free Press. [Paris: Alcan, 1922.]

Ernst, Maurice. 1966. "Postwar Economic Growth in Eastern Europe." In *New Directions in the Soviet Economy,* Part IV. Joint Economic Committee, Congress of the United States. Washington, D.C.: Government Printing Office.

Europäischen Gemeinschaften. Statistiches Amt. [European Communities. Statistical Office.] 1972. *Sozialkonten, 1962–70.* Luxemburg.

Feldman, Gerald D. 1966. *Army, Industry, and Labor in Germany, 1914–1918.* Princeton, N.J.: Princeton University Press.

Fisher, Paul. 1971. "Developments and Trends in Social Security throughout the World, 1967–69." *International Social Security Association Review* 1: 3–34.

Form, William H., and Joan Huber. 1971. "Income, Race and the Ideology of Political Efficacy." *University of Illinois Bulletin* 69 (November 12): 659–688.

Fox, Thomas, and S. M. Miller. 1965. "Occupational Stratification and Mobility: Intra-Country Variations." *Studies in Comparative International Development* 1: 1–10.

Free, Lloyd A., and Hadley Cantril. 1967. *The Political Beliefs of Americans: A Study of Public Opinion.* New Brunswick, N.J.: Rutgers University Press.

Galenson, Walter. 1968. "Social Security and Economic Development: A Quantitative Approach." *Industrial and Labor Relations Review* 21 (June): 559–569.

Glazer, Nathan. 1971. "Paradoxes of Health Care." *The Public Interest* 22 (Winter): 62–77.

Gordon, Margaret S. 1963. *The Economics of Welfare Policies.* New York: Columbia University Press.

———. 1967. "The Case for Earnings-Related Social Security Benefits Restated." In *Old Age Income Assurance, Part II: The Aged Population and Retirement Income Programs.* Joint Economic Committee, Congress of the United States. Washington, D.C.: Government Printing Office.

———. 1970. "Aging and Income Security in the U.S.: 35 Years after the Social Security Act." *The Gerontologist* 10 (Winter): 23–31.

Goudsblom, Johan. 1967. *Dutch Society.* New York: Random House.

Gouldner, Alvin W. 1970. *The Coming Crisis of Western Sociology.* New York: Basic Books.

Greve, John. 1971. *Voluntary Housing in Scandinavia: A Study of Denmark, Norway, and Sweden.* Birmingham: Centre for Urban and Regional Studies, University of Birmingham.

Gulick, Charles A. 1948. *Austria from Hapsburg to Hitler.* 2 Vols. Berkeley and Los Angeles: University of California Press.

Hagen, Everett E., and Oli Hawrylyshyn. 1969. "Analysis of World Income and Growth, 1955–1965." *Economic Development and Cultural Change* 18 (October): Part II.

Hansen, W. Lee, and Burton A. Weisbrod. 1969. "The Distribution of Costs and Direct Benefits of Public Higher Education: The Case of California." *Journal of Human Resources* 4 (Spring): 176–191.

Heise, D. R. 1969. "Problems in Path Analysis and Causal Inference." In *Sociological Methodology 1969,* edited by Edgar F. Borgatta. San Francisco: Jossey-Bass.

Horlick, Max. 1970. "Earnings Replacement Rate of Old-Age Benefits: An International Comparison." *Social Security Bulletin* 33 (March): 3–16.

Hurwitz, Samuel J. 1949. *State Intervention in Great Britain: A Study of Economic Control and Social Response, 1914–1919.* New York: Columbia University Press.

Hyman, Herbert H. 1953. "The Value Systems of Different Classes: A Social Psychological Contribution to the Analysis of Stratification." In *Class, Status and Power: A Reader in Social Stratification,* edited by Reinhard Bendix and S. M. Lipset. Glencoe, Illinois: Free Press.

Janda, Kenneth. 1970. "Measuring Issue Orientations of Parties Across Nations." ICPP Reports No. 7. Evanston, Illinois: International Comparative Political Parties Project, Northwestern University. Unpublished report.

Jencks, Christopher, et al. 1972. *Inequality: A Reassessment of the Effect of Family and Schooling in America.* New York: Basic Books.

Kallen, David J., and Dorothy Miller. 1971. "Public Attitudes toward Welfare." *Social Work* 16 (July): 83–90.

Katona, George, B. Strumpel, and E. Zahn. 1971. *Aspirations and Affluence.* New York: McGraw-Hill.

Klein, Rudolph. 1973. "National Health Service: After Reorganisation." *The Political Quarterly* 44 (July–September): 316–328.

Kuznets, Simon. 1950. *Shares of Upper Income Groups in Income and Savings.* New York: National Bureau of Economic Research (Occasional Paper 35).

———. 1953. *Shares of Upper Income Groups in Income and Savings.* New York: National Bureau of Economic Research.

Land, Kenneth C. 1969. "Principles of Path Analysis." In *Sociological Methodology 1969,* edited by Edgar F. Borgatta. San Francisco: Jossey-Bass.

Lasswell, Harold D. 1941. "The Garrison State." *American Journal of Sociology* 46 (January): 455–468.

Linz, Juan. 1964. "An Authoritarian Regime: Spain." In *Cleavages, Ideologies, and Party Systems,* edited by E. Allardt and Y. Luttunen. Helsinki: Westermarck Society.

Lipset, Seymour M. 1972. "Social Mobility and Equal Opportunity." *Public Interest* 29 (Fall): 90–108.

Litwack, Leon F. 1961. *North of Slavery: The Negro in the Free States, 1790–1860.* Chicago: University of Chicago Press.

McGranahan, Donald V. 1970. "Social Planning and Social Security." Geneva: International Institute of Labour Studies, Bulletin No. 7.

Mallory, Walter H., ed. 1950–65. *Political Handbook and Atlas of the World: Parliaments, Parties, and Press.* 16 vols. New York: Harper and Row, for the Council on Foreign Relations.

Marshall, T. H. 1964. *Class, Citizenship, and Social Development.*
Garden City, N.Y.: Doubleday.
————. 1965. *Social Policy in the 20th Century.* London: Hutchinson
University Library.
Marx, Gary T. 1967. *Protest and Prejudice.* New York: Harper and
Row.
Maxwell, James A. 1969. *Financing State and Local Governments.*
Rev. ed. Washington, D.C.: Brookings Institution.
Melman, Seymour. 1965. *Our Depleted Society.* New York: McGraw-
Hill.
Miller, Glenn W., et al. 1963. *Use of and Attitude toward the Ohio
Bureau of Unemployment Compensation: A Research Report.*
The Research Foundation, Ohio State University.
Murray, Janet. 1971. "Living Arrangements of People Aged 65 and
Older: Findings from the 1968 Survey of the Aged." *Social
Security Bulletin* 34 (September): 3–14.
Myrdal, Gunnar. 1960. *Beyond the Welfare State.* New Haven: Yale
University Press.
Nagai, Michio. 1971. *Higher Education in Japan: Its Take-off and
Crash.* Tokyo: University of Tokyo Press.
Nicholson, J. L. 1974. "The Distribution and Redistribution of Income
in the United Kingdom." In *Poverty, Inequality and Class
Structure*, edited by Dorothy Wedderburn. Cambridge: Cam-
bridge University Press.
Nimitz, Nancy. 1962. *Soviet National Income and Product, 1956–1958.*
Memorandum RM-3112-PR. Santa Monica, Calif.: U.S. Depart-
ment of the Air Force. Project Rand.
Oakley, Stewart. 1966. *The Story of Sweden.* London: Faber and
Faber.
Organisation for Economic Cooperation and Development. 1971.
Development of Higher Education, 1950–1967. Vol. 2, Analytical
Report. Paris: OECD.
————. 1972. *Expenditure Trends in OECD Countries, 1960–1980.*
Paris: OECD.
Orshansky, Mollie. 1965a. "Counting the Poor: Another Look at the
Poverty Profile." *Social Security Bulletin* 28 (January): 3–29.
————. 1965b. "Who's Who Among the Poor: A Demographic View
of Poverty." *Social Security Bulletin* 28 (July): 3–32.
Peacock, Alan T., and Jack Wiseman. 1961. *The Growth of Public
Expenditure in the United Kingdom.* Princeton: Princeton Univer-
sity Press.
Pechman, Joseph A. 1970. "The Distributional Effects of Public Higher

Education in California." *The Journal of Human Resources* 5 (Summer): 361–370.

————. 1971. *Federal Tax Policy*. Rev. ed. New York: Norton.

Pechman, Joseph A., Henry J. Aaron, and Michael K. Taussig. 1968. *Social Security: Perspectives for Reform*. Washington, D.C.: Brookings Institution.

Perrin, Guy. 1969. "The Future of Social Security." *International Social Security Review* 1: 3–27.

Piven, Frances F., and Richard A. Cloward. 1971. *Regulating the Poor: The Functions of Public Welfare*. New York: Random House (Pantheon).

Poignant, Raymond. 1969. *Education and Development in Western Europe, the United States, and the U.S.S.R.: A Comparative Study*. New York: Teachers College Press, Columbia University.

Pryor, Frederic L. 1968. *Public Expenditures in Communist and Capitalist Nations*. Homewood, Illinois: Irwin.

Rein, Martin. 1969. "Social Class and the Utilization of Medical Care Service." *Journal of the American Hospital Association* 43 (July): 43–54.

Riesman, David, and Gerald Grant. 1973. "Evangelism, Egalitarianism, and Educational Reform." *Minerva* 11 (July): 296–317.

Rimlinger, G. 1966. "Welfare Politics and Economic Development." *Journal of History* 26 (December): 556–571.

————. 1971. *Welfare Policy and Industrialization in Europe, America, and Russia*. New York: Wiley.

Ritz, Joseph P. 1966. *The Despised Poor: Newburgh's War on Welfare*. Boston: Beacon Press.

Rositi, Franco, ed. 1973. *Social Rationality and Information Technology: Description and Critique of the Technocratic Utopia*. Milan: Edizioni de Communità. Vol. 3.

Russett, Bruce M. 1970. *What Price Vigilance?* New Haven: Yale University Press.

Rutkevich, M. N., and F. R. Filippov. 1970. "Social Sources of Recruitment of the Intelligentsia." In *Sotsial'nye peremeshcheniia* by M. N. Rutkevich and F. R. Filippov. Moscow: Mysl' Publishing House.

Rytina, Joan H., William H. Form, and John Pease. 1970. "Income and Stratification Ideology: Beliefs about the American Opportunity Structure." *American Journal of Sociology* 75 (January): 703–716.

Schiltz, Michael A. 1970. *Public Attitudes toward Social Security, 1935–1965*. Washington, D.C.: Social Security Administration, Office of Research and Statistics, Research Report No. 33.

Selznick, Gertrude J., and Stephen Steinberg. 1969. *The Tenacity of*
Prejudice: Anti-Semitism in Contemporary America. New York: Harper and Row.
Shanas, Ethel, et al. 1968. *Old People in Three Industrial Societies*. New York: Atherton Press.
Simmons, R. G., and M. Rosenberg. 1971. "Functions of Children's Perceptions of the Stratification System." *American Sociological Review* 36 (April): 235–249.
Smith, Adam. 1937. *An Inquiry into the Nature and Causes of the Wealth of Nations*. (Modern Library ed.) New York: Random House. [5th ed., 1789.]
Solow, Robert M. 1960. "Income Inequality Since the War." In *Post-War Economic Trends in the United States*, edited by Ralph E. Freeman. New York: Harper.
Spitaels, Guy, et al. 1971. *La Comparaison Internationale Allemagne-France-Italie-Pays-Bas*. Brussels: Université Libre de Bruxelles.
Steiner, Gilbert Y. 1971. *The State of Welfare*. Washington, D.C.: Brookings Institution.
Szymanski, Albert. 1973. "Military Spending and Economic Stagnation." *American Journal of Sociology* 79 (July): 1–14.
Taira, Koji, and Peter Kilby. 1969. "Differences in Social Security Development in Selected Countries." *International Social Security Review* 22: 139–153.
Titmuss, Richard M. 1958. *Essays on "The Welfare State."* London: Allen and Unwin.
Trow, Martin. 1972. *The Expansion and Transformation of Higher Education*. Morristown, N.J.: General Learning Press.
United Kingdom. Central Statistical Office and Department of Health and Social Security. 1972. "The Incidence of Taxes and Social Service Benefits in 1967." *Economic Trends* 220. London: Her Majesty's Stationery Office.
United Nations. Economic Commission for Europe. 1958. *Financing of Housing in Europe*. Geneva: UNECE.
———. 1966. *Major Long-Term Problems of Government Housing and Related Problems*. New York: UNECE.
———. 1967a. *Annual Bulletin of Housing and Building Statistics*. Geneva: UNECE.
———. 1967b. *Incomes in Postwar Europe: A Study of Policies, Growth and Distribution* (Economic Survey of Europe in 1965: Part 2). Geneva: UNECE.
———. 1968. *The Housing Situation and Perspectives for Long-Term Housing Requirements in European Countries*. Geneva: UNECE.

United Nations. Economic Commission for Europe. 1970. *Annual Bulletin of Housing and Building Statistics for Europe* 13 (1969). New York: UNECE.

United Nations. Statistical Office. 1966. *Yearbook of National Account Statistics.* New York: UNSO.

———. 1971. *Demographic Yearbook 1970.* New York: UNSO.

United States. Bureau of the Census. 1967. *Government Finances in 1965–66.* Series GF, No. 13. Washington, D.C.: Government Printing Office.

United States. Department of Health, Education and Welfare. 1971. *Social Security Programs Throughout the World.* Washington, D.C.: Social Security Administration, Office of Research and Statistics, Research Report No. 40.

———. December, 1973. *New Jersey Graduated Work Incentive Experiment: Summary Report.*

Watts, Harold W., and Glen G. Cain. 1974. "Basic Labor Supply Findings from the Urban Experiment (New Jersey–Pennsylvania)." Paper presented at the annual meeting of the American Economic Association, New York, Dec. 30, 1973. Findings published in *Journal of Human Resources* 9 (Spring, 1974).

Wendt, Paul. 1962. *Housing Policy—the Search for Solutions: A Comparison of the United Kingdom, Sweden, West Germany and the United States Since World War II.* Berkeley and Los Angeles: University of California Press.

Wildavsky, Aaron. 1964. *The Politics of the Budgetary Process.* Boston: Little, Brown.

Wilensky, Harold L. 1960. "Work, Careers, and Social Integration." *International Social Science Journal* 12 (Fall): 543–560.

———. 1961. "Orderly Careers and Social Participation: The Impact of Work History on Social Integration in the Middle Mass." *American Sociological Review* 26 (August): 521–539.

———. 1964. "Mass Society and Mass Culture: Interdependence or Independence?" *American Sociological Review* 29 (April): 173–197.

———. 1965. "The Problems and Prospects of the Welfare State." In *Industrial Society and Social Welfare* by H. L. Wilensky and C. N. Lebeaux. Enlarged paperback ed. Glencoe, Illinois: Free Press.

———. 1966a. "Measures and Effects of Social Mobility." In *Social Structure and Mobility in Economic Development,* edited by Neil J. Smelser and Seymour M. Lipset. Chicago: Aldine.

Wilensky, Harold L. 1966b. "Work as a Social Problem." In *Social Problems*, edited by Howard S. Becker. New York: Wiley.

———. 1967. *Organizational Intelligence: Knowledge and Policy in Government and Industry.* New York: Basic Books.

———. 1972. "Intelligence, Crises, and Foreign Policy: Reflections on the Limits of Rationality." In *Surveillance and Espionage in a Free Society*, edited by Richard H. Blum. New York: Praeger.

Wilensky, Harold L., and C. N. Lebeaux. 1958. *Industrial Society and Social Welfare.* New York: Russell Sage Foundation.

Index

32/105